CANOE-FISHING NEW YORK RIVERS AND STREAMS

By M. Paul Keesler

Artwork by William J. Davis
Illustrations by
William J. Davis and David W. Hamilton

EASY CANOEING
GREAT FISHING

CANOE-FISHING NEW YORK RIVERS AND STREAMS
by
M. Paul Keesler

Copyright © 1995

Artwork and Illustrations by William Davis
Illustrations by David W. Hamilton
Photographs by the author

**LIBRARY OF CONGRESS
CATALOG CARD NUMBER: 95-75842**

Keesler, M. Paul
Prospect, New York
Mid-York Sportsman Inc.
Prospect, New York

ISBB 0-9645372-1-4

Price: $19.95 US

**North Country Books, Inc.
Distributor
18 Irving Place, Utica, NY 13501**

CONTENTS

DEDICATION:
To the Native Americans who created the canoe

ACKNOWLEDGMENTS

I owe a special debt of gratitude to my wife, Gertrude for her patience and perseverance for the past three years, and for reading and rereading every part of this book; to William (Bill) Davis for his artwork and illustrations; to David Hamilton for his illustrations; to the good people at Canterbury Press for helping me prepare text and photographs; to Jack Hasse for reviewing the chapter on fish species; to Bill Hollister for reviewing the chapter on wildlife species; to Bob McNitt for reviewing every chapter, and to Sheila Orlin and Rob Igoe of North Country Books for sharing their book publishing knowledge and experience .

Not everyone can mix picture-taking with canoe-fishing, so the following individuals who joined me on trips across New York State—and sometimes had to stop for me to take pictures when the fish were biting—deserve special recognition: Joe Hackett, Mike Seymour, Paul Gibaldi, Denny Gillen, Pete Hornbeck, Bob McNitt, Ron Gugnacki, Dave Hamilton, Emlen Hamilton, Mark Eychner, J. Michael Kelly, Gordon Potter, Glenn Sapir, Tom Murray, Mike Warren, John Pitarresi and my daughter, Bridget Keesler-Sherline.

Invaluable information and guidance were provided by many individuals who work (or worked) for the New York State Department of Environmental Conservation. Among them are: Bruce Shupp, Wayne Elliot, Bob Angyal, Ron Pierce, Doug Carlson, Dave Lemon, Les Wedge and Tom Murray.

A very special thanks to Lou Hoffman and the Northwoods Publishing team, and to Sue Owens at the Prospect, NY office of the **NEW YORK SPORTSMAN** magazine for relieving me of magazine publishing duties and responsibilities, so I had the time, resources and energy to make this book a reality.

And finally to my parents Ruth-Blair Keesler and Milton L.Keesler for instilling in me a love for the out-of-doors and a desire to learn what's around the next bend, I offer my undying gratitude and love.

FORWARD

Paul Keesler and I share a common love for being in the great outdoors. The beautiful visual and symphonic masterpieces that nature offers us have never been duplicated by man. So, with such a common bond, it was also only natural that our life-paths would cross. As an avid reader and fan of his beloved publication, the *NEW YORK SPORTSMAN*, I felt that I knew Paul long before he knew me. When he published one of my stories in 1979, we finally met face-to-face. We became immediate friends.

Amidst the many outdoor interests we discovered we shared, one of the stronger was canoe-fishing; both of us had been enjoying this underutilized, enjoyable and productive activity for most of our lives. In the years since that fateful meeting, we've spent countless hours and miles sharing a canoe. And, we've become more like brothers than close friends, probably because of it; sharing our lives, the ups and downs, joys and tragedies.

For, when one wants to truly think clearly—to cut to the heart of any matter, major or minor—there are precious few places better than in a canoe on one of God's streams or rivers.

When Paul told me of his plans to write this book, I was both elated and, I must admit, a bit jealous; elated that such a badly needed book would finally be available for sportsmen, and a smidgen jealous that it would be Paul who would be the one to step forward and do it. But, being an outdoor writer myself, when I considered the amount of work necessary to accomplish such a literary feat, my jealousy quickly faded.

Paul is definitely qualified—and no doubt the right one—to write this book; he's canoe-fished all over New York State and knows countless streams and rivers—and the fish and best fishing techniques there—intimately. His journalistic nature also prompts him to seek out and garner advice from those who are most qualified to know what he may not yet know about each water.

As you read these pages, note that he is also not the type of writer who fictionalizes, based on what any given water's "potential fishing" might be. If the fishing was slow during the trip Paul's writing about, he reports it as such. And, as both a reader and writer, I truly enjoy such honesty—especially in an age when too many writers seem tempted to glorify every account into a best case, but often fictional, scenario.

Paul asked me to review the galleys and critique what he'd written. Armed with a sharpened editor's pencil, I did. But try as I might, I could find precious little to add, change or delete. He has done an outstanding job and, I feel, one that will provide many benefits to those who read the book. I also suspect—because of its wealth of information, maps, etc.—it will become as much an ongoing, long-term reference text for readers as it will merely a quick and enjoyable read.

A book such as this is long overdue. I'm very happy that what you're about to read is representative of the quality, thoroughness, accuracy and honesty such a milestone publication deserves.

Bob McNitt
Editor
NEW YORK SPORTSMAN MAGAZINE

INTRODUCTION

There are literally thousands of miles of streams in New York State where the canoeing is easy and the fishing is exciting... if you know how and where.

Every time I launch a canoe on a New York river or stream it's the start of a new adventure. I'm not into the haystacks and curls of roaring water, so my adventures are the feel of a canoe in easywater, the sights and sounds of flora and fauna, and the strikes of hungry fish ... fish that seldom see a lure or bait.

Canoe-fishing on a free-flowing stream is both relaxing and exciting to me. Tensions flow from my body and mind with the first stroke of the paddle. At the same time I get high on gliding through an almost magical world of trees, plants and flowers where an amazing variety of birds and other wildlife abound even on the most urban streams.

As roadside parking areas disappear, I cast to waters that few fishermen have even seen. Here the trout, bass, walleye, northern pike and other stream-fish are more wild and less wary than their roadside cousins. They hit hard and fight hard when a lure or bait looks like an easy meal.

I've been canoeing and fishing New York State rivers and streams for 30 years and I just can't get enough of it. I canoe-fish spring, summer and fall, and fish for trout, bass, pike and walleye. You'd think that would be enough to satisfy any canoe-fishing nut. Nope. I can always use just one more "fix" before the rivers ice up.

On a recent November day when a break in the weather produced a couple of hours of sunshine and temperatures above 45 degrees, my wife, Gert and I canoed a short stretch of West Canada Creek for just one hour. We saw 50 Canada geese, two mallards, five mergansers, a great blue heron, an osprey and several species of song birds. I caught a two pound fallfish, lost a fair-size smallmouth bass and had several other fish sock my lure. Except at the bridge where we put in and the parking area where we took out, we never saw another human being.

Not every outing is as eventful as that hour but canoe-fishing is way up there with the very best outdoor adventures. Funny thing, not many people have even tried it.

Most fishermen do not canoe
Most canoeists do not fish

To me canoeing and fishing go together like peanut butter and jelly, or ham and eggs, yet most fishermen do not canoe and most canoeists do not fish. Many fishermen consider canoeing too dangerous and many canoeists think that fishing is too difficult or just plain boring. By looking at just part of the picture they are correct on all accounts. Canoeing in white water is dangerous and some kinds of fishing are difficult and boring beyond belief.

I've experienced the excitement of running a roaring rapids in a canoe, but I have no desire to make a habit of it. I much prefer a stream that offers quiet water, fast runs, riffles, short, safe rapids and enough obstacles to make it interesting ... and hold fish. There are thousands of miles of such streams in New York, and it's easy to canoe-fish them if you know how and where.

That's what this book is all about.

Whiteface Mountain overlooks this stretch of the Ausable River where Joe Hackett and I caught rainbow, brown and brook trout.

CHAPTER 1

WHAT KIND OF CANOE

I've fished from canoes ranging in size from a tiny 10-footer that weighs a mere 15 pounds to a giant 35-foot war canoe that weighs more than 250 pounds. The small canoe is a sit-on-the-bottom, surprisingly stable craft for one person to canoe-fish streams and ponds while carrying a minimum of gear. The war canoe is ultra stable, can carry plenty of gear and has enough room for three fly fishermen to cast without interference ... on large rivers and lakes.

While fishing from both of these canoes was great fun, I prefer a stable canoe that handles well on free-flowing streams and provides room for two anglers with all the gear they need for a day of canoe-fishing.

A wide-bottomed canoe is ideal for canoe-fishing easywater, so if you don't already own a canoe, look for one of the many models that are designed for stability. A 14 to 17-foot canoe with a beam (width) of 35 to 40 inches is about right for two fishermen. The longer canoe is best if you plan to carry camping gear or another angler.

Serious canoeists—the ones who race, run rapids, or paddle across wave tossed lakes—must consider such canoe design factors as symmetry, tumblehome (inward curve of the sides), rocker (fore and aft curve of the keel line), but the primary consideration for canoe-fishing rivers and streams is the cross section hull design.

The two hull designs I recommend for canoe-fishing easywater are the flat-bottomed and the shallow "V" bottom. Generally a flat bottomed canoe feels (and is) the most stable in relatively calm water. However, it can be difficult to maneuver in fast water, and can flip over in high waves.

The shallow "V" bottomed canoe can ride —and cut through— the waves, and it paddles, handles and tracks (travels in a straight line) like a dream. However, it feels (and is) more tippy than the flat-bottomed canoe. Actually it's much more stable than it seems,

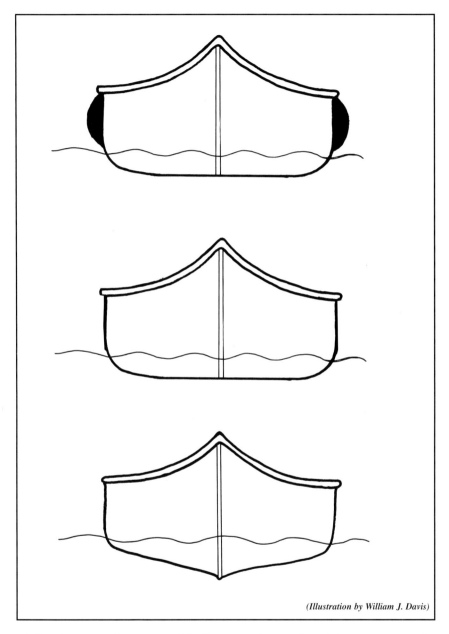

(Illustration by William J. Davis)

A flat-bottomed canoe with foam pads on the sides is extremely stable but difficult to paddle long distances and against the current. The flat-bottomed canoe without pads feels very stable and it's easier to paddle without the side-pads. The shallow "V" bottom canoe is easy to paddle and control, but it's "initial" stability makes it feel tippy, especially to first-time canoeists.

Wide bottomed canoes are ideal for canoe-fishing. Some of the canoes I have fished from—left to right—17' Grumman aluminum, 16' Mad River Explorer kevlar, 15' Coleman polyethylene, 14' Sportspal aluminum/foam clad and a 12' Watersport aluminum foam clad.

Canoe Equipment that can make the difference—left to right: anchor and rope, sneakers (summer), hip boots (spring and fall), seat back rest, life vests (adult), life vest (child), pack basket, cartop canoe carriers, cooler, small tackle box, fishing vest, fishing rods, fishing net, paddles, binoculars, hat and rain jacket.

having an initial and "secondary" stability that allows the canoe to tip a little from side to side but provides increased stability at greater side-to-side angles.

For canoe-fishing easywater the practical difference is that the flat-bottomed canoe is a very stable craft to fish from, but it's not as easy to paddle long stretches of stillwater, or to paddle back upstream to retrieve snagged lures, as is the shallow "V".

FAT STUBBY AND FOAM CLAD

If you don't care about looks or ease of paddling, one of those fat, stubby canoes with the foam pads on the sides are ideal for canoe-fishing. I bought a 14-foot Sportspal years ago and have never regretted it. It's lightweight—less than 50 pounds—and very quiet for an aluminum canoe because of the foam on the inside. I have also used a similarly constructed canoe that is only 12 feet long and I like it almost as much as my 14-footer.

The model I have has seats with a backrest made of high density foam that sit on the floor. They get very uncomfortable after awhile. (Newer models offer conventional seats, but are a few pounds heavier.) The combination of sitting so close to the bottom and the foam pads on each side make the canoe extremely stable ... and difficult to paddle on long stretches of stillwater.

FIBERGLASS AND PLASTIC

My first canoe was made by a company that made fiberglass porta-johns. I canoe-fished and canoe-camped streams and lakes and ran rapids with that 15-footer, and it was great until I hurt my back and couldn't handle it's 85 pounds by myself.

Today, fiberglass canoes are still excellent for canoe-fishing. They are quiet, tough, easy to maintain, come in all shapes and sizes, and are relatively inexpensive. But, they are heavy. If you always fish with a partner or have no problem handling an 80-pound canoe—putting it on and taking it off your car—fiberglass is the way to go.

Plastics have revolutionized the canoe making industry. They range from the same polyethylene that's used to make liquid detergent bottles, to super tough Royalex to space-age Kevlar materials. They are strong, lightweight and usually spring back to their original shape soon after they encounter an immovable object ... like a rock. They are also slippery, so they slide over underwater rocks that love to take a bite out of aluminum.

All things being equal Polyethylene is the least expensive, Royalex is the toughest and Kevlar is the lightest. Canoe manufacturers use combinations of these materials, plus fiberglass, plastic foam, metals and wood to create canoes that vary considerably in durability, flexibility, weight and beauty.

ALUMINUM

Most rental outfits prefer aluminum canoes because they take a beating and last, and last, and last. Campfires can't melt them, repairs are easy and the wide-bottomed models are extremely stable. I've canoe-fished from a number of beaten and battered aluminum canoes that had been in the same family for many years. Only one drawback, they are noisy. Drop a paddle or a tackle box in them and you can forget about fishing that spot for awhile. Many fishermen and hunters line the inside of their canoes with outdoor carpet to cut down on the noise. It works, but adds weight to the canoe.

WOOD AND CANVAS

Many beautiful canoes are made of wood or wood and canvas. They require a great deal of care and are very expensive.

NEW OR USED

A new canoe can cost anywhere from a few hundred dollars to a couple of thousand dollars depending on materials, construction, size and manufacturer. Used canoes can be had for a couple hundred bucks, sometimes less.

The advantage of a new canoe is that you can buy exactly what you want. If you can afford it and want a beautiful, lightweight, well made, wide-bottomed canoe, consider buying one made of kevlar with hardwood trim and seats. A number of manufacturers make such canoes, including Mad River and Old Town. If on the other hand beauty and ease of handling is not your thing, but incredible stability and quiet is what you want, take a close look at the canoes made by Sportspal. And if you're looking for a canoe that can take a beating, consider buying one made of aluminum or super-tough plastics. Grumman makes aluminum canoes right here in New York State.

USED BUT NOT ABUSED

Canoe-fishing doesn't demand a special canoe, so almost any wide bottomed variety will suffice. So, finding a used canoe that will take you down easywater streams is not difficult. There are literally thousands of used canoes out there if you know where to look.

The obvious place to look is in the classified section of your local newspaper. Some not so obvious places are at marinas, boat dealers and sport shops. They sell canoes they take as trade-ins. Outfitters and canoe rental outfits sometimes sell canoes when they replace damaged units. I recently purchased a beaten and battered 17-foot Grumman for $100 from a canoe rental outfit that was going out of business. It's not pretty but the fish don't care.

Another good way to locate used canoes is to keep your eyes and ears open. There are thousands of used canoes stored in barns, garages, camps and in backyards, that have not been used in years. If you see or hear of such canoes, don't be afraid to ask if they're for sale. When I asked a friend about the two canoes in his backyard that were covered with leaves, he gave me one of them with the stipulation that I had to clean it up and use it. I've done both.

Most used aluminum canoes are still in good shape even if they are scratched and dented, but fiberglass and plastic canoes deteriorate if left outside in the sun of summer and the cold of winter. Look them over carefully for delaminations, cracks and deep cuts. Check the wood trim for rot by pushing your fingernail or a small knife into discolored areas. Use the canoe to check for leaks and weak spots in the hull.

Don't forget to ask if there are paddles that come with the canoe. Usually the paddles are stored out of the weather and are still serviceable.

When you get the canoe home, give it a bath with a mild detergent and water. After it dries, make necessary repairs, replace defective hardware, refinish the wood trim and apply a coat of paste wax to the outside of the canoe. Wax does wonders for the looks of a fiberglass or plastic canoe.

This assortment of lures is a good starter kit for canoe-fishing rivers and streams. Left—spinner bait, beetle spin. Center—Phoebe spoon; Vibrax, Mepps, Panther Martin spinners; curly tailed plastic jig. Right—floating Rapala imitation minnows and Rebel crayfish imitation plugs.

The best way to locate streams is with "New York Stream Map & Location Guide"; the best way to locate put in and take out points is with the "DeLorme New York State Gazetteer", and the best way to locate rapids, dams and obstructions is with an area topographical map.

CHAPTER 2

EQUIPMENT YOU'LL NEED (OR LIKE TO HAVE)

It's easy to fill a canoe to the brim with nice-to-have gear that will make life easy and fun on the river. Of course the fun ends when you have to load all that gear in your canoe, portage it a few times and then put it back in your vehicle for the trip home. On the other hand, the spartan approach can make canoe-fishing downright uncomfortable and even dangerous.

The trick is to bring what you need ... plus a little more. For instance, for a day of fishing on a free-flowing stream, with two in a canoe, you'll **need** two paddles, two flotation devices (life vests are best), a canteen of water, two fishing rods, tackle and bait, a first aid kit, a roll of duct tape (for canoe and tackle repairs), and a canoe carrier and tie-down ropes for at least one vehicle.

Life will be easier and a lot more fun if you also bring: a cooler to carry drinks and eats, back rests, an extra paddle, an anchor with rope, a pack basket, rain gear, sun screen, extra fishing rods, a net, a pair of binoculars, and canoe carriers and ropes for two vehicles. And, if you're canoe-fishing long stretches of stillwater, a small outboard motor could save the day and a lot of time and effort.

WHAT'S NECESSARY (TWO IN A CANOE)

PADDLES

Two paddles are a must. No need to get fancy with bent-handle speed paddles, but don't go cheap either. Better to buy good used paddles than new discount store varieties. A 55-inch paddle will work just fine for most people, but the way to determine the best paddle length for you is to sit in a canoe and measure the distance between the bill of your cap and the water, and then add the length of the paddle blade.

LIFE VESTS

A flotation device for each person in a canoe (or any boat) is the law in New York State, but a good life vest that zips up the front is more sensible. Some manufacturers make life vests that double as fishing vests. Make sure these vests can be adjusted to fit properly. Never put adult vests on small children. They can slide right off them.

CANOE CARRIERS

A canoe rack for your vehicle is a good idea if you have your canoe on-top most of the time, but the foam pad carriers made for canoes and small boats are convenient. They don't mar the vehicle's finish and can be moved from one car to another with ease. (They don't work on pickup trucks or on some vans.) I keep my pads with tie-down ropes in a plastic bag. If the vehicle parked downstream doesn't have a canoe rack, I carry the pads-bag in the canoe.

An entire book could be written on the variety of racks that are used to haul canoes and boats. Some of them are designed especially for canoes, but most are modified ladder or luggage racks that clamp to the vehicle's roof gutter or drip edge. Depending on the shape of the rack's cross bars, carpet can be wrapped around the rack or a heater hose slipped over it to keep from marring the canoe and to reduce side to side slippage.

When I had just one canoe, I cut 2x2's to fit and cradle my canoe and bolted them to ladder racks. I used that rig for years and it worked perfectly.

I prefer 3\8-inch nylon rope for tie-downs. It's tough, doesn't rot and it stretches just enough to allow me to pull it tight and tie it off. If the knot slips a bit, no problem, there is still plenty of tension to hold the canoe securely. All my tie-down ropes are cut to length and the ends melted to stop fraying. One end has a permanent loop in it, the other is the tie-end.

A canoe-fishing buddy ties a loop in each tie-down rope about two feet above the tie-end, so he can run the rope back through it and cinch the line before tying it off. I've also seen some excellent tie-downs using straps equipped with ratchet-tighteners.

It's a good idea to tie both the front and the rear of the canoe as well as two places across the belly. It's difficult to find places to tie to the front and rear of newer vehicles and even the old time bumpers can cut a rope, so "S" hooks are great for securing ropes

A 3/8-inch nylon rope is excellent for canoe tie-downs. It doesn't rot and it stretches enough to hold the canoe securely even if the knot slips a little. Tying a loop about two feet above the tie-end to run the rope through it for a tight cinch before tying it off can prevent knot slippage.

(Illustration by William J. Davis)

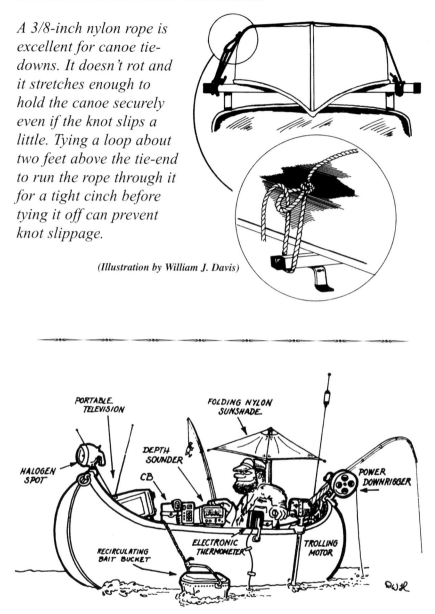

(cartoon by Dave Hamilton)

It's tempting to bring all the comforts of home and your modern fishing equipment with you on a canoe-fishing trip, but the fun ends when you have to pack and portage all that gear. The trick is to bring what you need ... plus a little more.

to the bumper or undercarriage. Heavy duty elastic cords with hooks on both ends also work well.

COOLERS

A cooler is not necessary, but for cold drinks and good eats, like sandwiches and fruit, it's a must for those hot and sunny days. I always bring along a cooler because it keeps things safe, dry and easy to handle. A well-iced cooler is also the best place for worms and the fish you keep. A small, single handle cooler is fine most of the time, but for long trips or when more capacity is needed for riverside feasts or exceptional take-home catches, a bigger two handle model is much better.

BACKSAVERS

In addition to life vests, fishing tackle, a net, cooler and thermos, there are a few good-to-have items that can make your outing more enjoyable and more successful. Number one is a canoe seat backrest. Until I started using these "backsavers", I had to get out of the canoe every hour or so to stretch. There are some simple, folding models on the market that work just fine. The Coleman company makes one that fits most canoe seats.

ANCHOR & ROPES

An anchor isn't a must for canoe-fishing, but it sure helps to keep you and your canoe near fish-holding water. A mushroom anchor is ideal but an old-time heavy window weight works great in most waters. Fifty feet of anchor rope is plenty.

Two 10-foot lengths of rope attached to or near the seats are great for tying the canoe to shoreline brush and trees within casting distance of fish havens. A spring clamp attached to the loose end makes this arrangement much more convenient.

PACK BASKET & WET BAGS

I prefer a pack basket to hold most of my gear, including a rain jacket, binoculars, camera, thermos, rain jacket, small first aid kit and an extra hat. I put my waterproof daypack in it or line it with a heavy duty plastic bag and tie it to the canoe. It's easy to get stuff out of and throw stuff into, and it keeps my gear off the bottom of the canoe ... which is always wet when you're canoe-fishing.

There are a number of plastic, heavy duty wet bags on the market that will keep your gear dry. One model attaches to the bottom of a canoe seat.

HIP BOOTS & SNEAKERS
When it's cold I wear hip boots and when it's warm I wear sneakers so I can wade when I have to. Even with sneakers I wear socks because they keep those mean little stones from getting to my feet.

DUCT TAPE
One item that should travel with every canoe-fisherman is a roll of duct tape. It's great for canoe repairs and doesn't do a bad job on waders and fishing rods.

CAMPING GEAR
Camping gear for canoe-fishermen can run the gamut from the spartan to the near luxurious, depending on the size of the canoe and canoeists, and the length and number of portages. I use the same gear I use for backpacking ... and then add a few luxuries like a large cooler filled with real food and beverages, a two-burner camp stove, a lantern and good size tarp. You'll find a detailed canoe-camping list in the back of the book.

OUTBOARD MOTOR & MOUNT
Another canoe-fishing luxury is a small outboard motor. On a free-flowing stream where you launch upstream and take out downstream, the current and your paddle-power are sufficient. But, on a slow-moving stream or stillwater, an outboard motor can save the day and increase fishing time considerably. It's also great for traveling upstream or down on many of our deeper rivers and streams.

An outboard motor should never be mounted on the side of the canoe. A canoe motor mount is a must. I've made a couple over the years from a length of pipe, a piece of 2X4 and some bolts, however, if you are not so inclined, there are a number of inexpensive models on the market. Two to three horsepower is plenty of motor, and one with the gas tank attached is easier to handle and portage. These little motors can vibrate quite a bit, especially at slow speeds, so check the mounting bolts often and use a piece of nylon rope as a safety "chain" just in case the motor decides to leave the canoe.

CHAPTER 3

HOW TO HANDLE A CANOE IN EASYWATER

A canoe—the right canoe—is very stable. The fact is a 16–17 foot, wide-bottomed canoe is difficult to tip over in easywater, and one of those fat stubby models with the foam pads on the sides is almost impossible to tip over. My son had to literally jump on the gunnel to flip our 14-foot Sportspal.

Of course that doesn't mean that a canoe is as stable as a bass boat. Far from it. Safety in a canoe—any canoe—requires a little common sense and some basic canoeing skills. Two common sense rules are: don't stand up in a canoe unless you're prepared to fall out, and the lower you are in a canoe the more stable it will be.

The easiest way to learn how to handle a canoe is to go with someone who's experienced, but you can go it alone. To get a "feel" for the canoe and learn some basic paddle strokes, take it out on a pond or lake. It's a good idea to have two people in most canoes to keep it level in the water. When the bow (front end) comes out of the water a canoe is almost impossible to control in even the slightest breeze ... and it gets very tipsy.

You can create the weight of a partner by putting rocks or a burlap bag full of sand in the bow of the canoe. Little or no weight is needed in the "front" of the canoe if you can sit or kneel in the bow position—facing the stern. In some models it's impossible to sit backwards in the bow position.

It's easy—and fun—to develop a repertoire of fancy paddle strokes, but just a few will do the trick nicely in easywater. The forward stroke comes quite naturally. Paddle forward on the left side of the canoe and it turns right. Paddle on the right side and it turns left. Simple enough. Trouble is, if you are alone in the canoe, you have to keep switching sides to keep from going in a circle. And, when you constantly switch sides the canoe zig–zags through the water. A simple outward turn of the paddle near the end of each stroke (that's a J–stroke) helps to counteract the turning force created by paddling on one side. To cut down on paddle noise don't lift the paddle out of the water all the way, turn it sideways when you draw it forward to begin another stroke.

With two in the canoe it's a whole lot easier. By paddling on the opposite side of the canoe, the bow paddler counteracts some of the turning force of the stern (rear) paddler. As both paddlers adjust to their individual strengths and develop canoeing skills, it becomes easier for the stern paddler to keep the canoe going in a straight line with very few J–strokes.

There are times when sharp turns are a must. Back paddling is very effective for this kind of maneuver. Back paddling is simple enough to understand, just try to paddle the canoe backwards without turning around in the canoe. Practice back paddling in calm water and perfect it in a slow-moving river or stream.

Even in easywater you have to learn to "read" the water to keep from getting hung up on a rock or log. Above water obstacles are usually easy to see, but those just under the surface are the real troublemakers. Look for the pockets of "white" water that boil or curl downstream from underwater rocks and logs in fast water. Remember the troublemaker is upstream from the white water.

Most of the time it's a good idea to avoid rapids altogether, but as your skills and confidence increases, most short rapids are easy to negotiate if you remember to steer for the V's that point downstream and avoid the V's that point upstream.

During high water periods such as spring runoff, trees that hang into the water and trees that fall into the water and pile up at the bends in many streams, can be very dangerous. These same trees that provide shade and cover for fish the rest of the year, can sweep a canoe clean or turn it over when the stream is high and rushing. Don't canoe-fish such streams early in the spring. Avoid "sweepers" anytime and take care when approaching piles of trees in fast water.

Most of the time it's easy to avoid dangerous areas by just paddling around them, usually on the other side of the stream. Sometimes the speed and direction of the current or the size of the stream or obstruction prevents such negotiation, so the best action is to stop the canoe. If you can't paddle to shore, **and** the water isn't

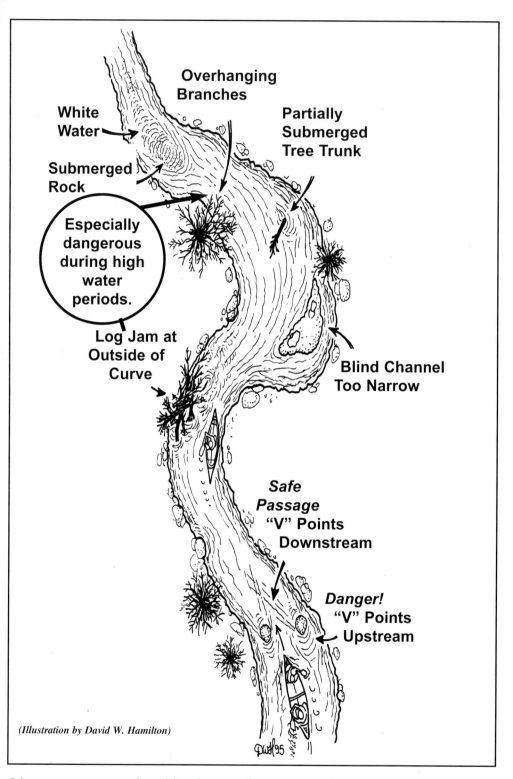

It's easy to stay out of trouble when you learn to "read the water" for underwater rocks and logs, and avoid trouble spots like piles of logs at sharp bends and branches that hang close to the water.

deep, just jump out of the canoe to stop it. I use this simple technique often. It works.

The "captain" in the stern has the most control over the direction of the canoe, so he calls the shots .... and does most of the work. The bow paddler, when required, sets the paddle rhythm, points out obstacles ahead, assists with sharp turns .... and does most of the fishing.

No canoe feels stable when you first get into it, especially if you sit in the bow, which is where new canoeists usually sit. Whether in the bow or stern, it doesn't take long to adjust to the feel of a canoe. Depending on experience—and experiences—that "tippy" feeling goes away in short order. It goes away much faster if you wear a life vest or jacket.

Every canoeist should have a life vest in the canoe, and wear it when the water is rough, deep or cold; if the canoeist is very young or very old, or if he feels uncomfortable not wearing one. New York State law requires an approved flotation device for each person in the canoe.

CHAPTER 4

FISHING TACKLE AND ACCESSORIES

There is more fishing tackle available today than there has ever been. Fishing catalogs as big as phone books are filled with pages of rods, reels, lines, lures, hooks, harnesses, baits, buckets, snaps, swivels and electronic gadgets that will help you catch fish in almost any situation. Deciding what fishing tackle to buy can be confusing and time consuming. Not to worry, the following information will get you off to a good start. Later you can tailor your tackle to the fish and waters you canoe-fish most often.

RODS AND REELS

Spinning gear is ideal for canoe-fishing. An ultralight outfit provides plenty of action on even the smallest fish and a real challenge when a big fish is at the end of the line. A medium action outfit has the backbone to cast big lures and bait and handle some fair size fish.

If one outfit is enough for you, the medium-action loaded with 6-pound test monofilament line is the best choice. It can cast a variety of lure sizes and subdue most stream fish.

A good all around arsenal is a 5 1/2-foot ultralight rod with a matching reel loaded with 6-pound line, and a 6–6 1/2-foot medium action rod with a reel loaded with 8-pound test line. A spare spool of 4-pound line for the ultralight will help to fool wary fish in clear water, and a spare spool of 10-pound line for the heavier reel will handle fish in heavy cover. There are times and places where heavier tackle may be required, but for most New York rivers and streams, these two outfits will do nicely.

Spincasting outfits also work well for canoe-fishing, and may be the tackle of choice for some fishermen because they are easier to use and relatively trouble free. They don't cast small lures and bait quite as far as spinning rigs, but that's not usually a problem canoe-fishing.

Fly-fishing from a moving canoe is not easy, and nowhere near as effective as spin fishing. However, a canoe can take a fly-fisherman to seldom fished water where he can fish from a stationary canoe or wade productive water.

There is no getting around the fact that it's great fun to catch a fish on a fly rod. At least one canoe-fisherman I know has mounted a spincast reel on a fly rod to create an outfit that casts lures and bait, and feels like a fly rod when there's a fish on.

TERMINAL TACKLE

The hooks, sinkers, snap swivels and leaders at the fish-end of the line are as important as the rods and reels at the other end.

Bait hooks ranging from Size-10 through 4 will cover most situations, with Size-6 being the best all around hook for fishing rivers and streams. Special hooks for big northern pike, trout and salmon can be added to the hook assortment as needed. Snelled hooks are fine but not really necessary when using monofilament fishing line. Quality hooks are well worth the extra cost.

Sinkers are clipped or otherwise attached to the fishing line to help the baited hook sink towards the bottom. The best type and weight of sinker depends on the size of the bait, current flow, depth of water and the species of fish. An assortment of split shot (BB through Size-5), clinch-on (1/16–1/4 ounce) will do for starters. Slip sinkers, casting sinkers and walking sinkers are very effective in some situations and can be added to the sinker assortment as needed.

Snap Swivels are used to attach lures to fishing line. They help prevent line twist and make changing lures a "snap". Sizes-5, 7 and 10 will cover most needs. Snap swivels are not recommended for some plugs and spinners because they affect lure action. The literature that comes with some lures explains the best way to attach lures to fishing line. Most notable of these is the Rapala "loop" knot.

Leaders can ruin lure action and scare fish. But, there is no denying that northern pike and pickerel have teeth sharp enough to cut fishing line. A two-foot piece of 20-pound test monofilament attached to the end of light-weight fishing line can prevent many cut-offs.

BOBBERS

Bobbers float on the surface of the water and are used to suspend bait and some lures off the bottom. Except for fishing big minnows for pike, thumb-size bobbers will do nicely.

LURE OR BAIT

It's more fun to catch fish on lures, but at times the only way to catch fish is on live bait. So, it's good to know how to fish both. The most effective lures are spoons, spinners, plugs and jigs ... or combinations thereof. The most popular live baits are minnows, crayfish and worms. The following information will put you into fish on rivers and streams, however, there are other baits and many other lures that will also take fish. If you have a lure or bait that works for you, fish it. Here are some of my favorites.

LURES

Spoons wiggle and wobble through the water and look like a small fish. My favorite is a gold Phoebe. It catches brown trout, smallmouth bass, pickerel and pike.

Spinners spin through the water and also look like small fish. My favorites are Mepps, Vibrax, Panther Martin, C.P. Swing and similar flashy lures. Again I like gold, but sometimes silver works better. They take trout, bass, pike, pickerel, walleye and fallfish.

Plugs swim, dive and wiggle though the water and look like small fish, crayfish and other fish food. My favorite for taking all kinds of fish is a floating Rapala minnow, in silver, gold and perch colors. The Rebel Crawfish and Wee Crawfish with the big diving lip in natural color is hard to beat for trout, bass and fallfish.

Jigs swim, dive, and jump through the water, depending on rod and reel action, and look like small fish, crayfish, insects, and leeches. My favorite is a 2-inch curly tail plastic jig in chartreuse, yellow, white, purple and black, on a round-headed jig in sizes 1/16 and 1/8- ounce. They take every kind of fish but are especially effective on bass, rock bass and walleye.

Combinations thereof are part spinner and part jig—spinner-jigs. Spinner baits and Beetle spins fall in this category. My favorite for smallmouth bass has a silver Colorado Blade and a chartreuse or yellow skirt or curly tail jig. Northern pike like a red and white blade and skirt.

LURE SIZES

The old adage, "Big lures for big fish." is often true. But don't bet on it. Sometimes a big fish will hit the tiniest lure and a tiny fish will attack a big lure. The shape of the lure and the size of the fish's mouth has something to do with the lures that trout and bass will hit. For instance a relatively small trout or bass will hit a slim and sleek Rapala minnow of almost any size, because it fits. So, a 4–5 inch Rapala minnow is a good choice for these fish. On the other hand a big spinner bait that takes largemouth bass is not very effective on even the biggest smallmouth bass. The smaller size spinner baits and spinner-jigs are deadly on smallmouths.

I had caught hundreds of smallmouth bass on the Rebel Crawfish, but they just didn't work on stream trout. But, when the Wee Crawfish came out, trout loved them. Trout have smaller mouths than bass.

Sometimes it's "what's for dinner" that makes the difference. If fish are feeding on small minnows, crayfish and insect larva, big lures seldom work.

Eating machines like northern pike and pickerel don't seem to care about the size of the lure. No matter what their size or the lure's size, if they're hungry or mad, they try to eat it. However, they are sight feeders, so bigger, flashier lures seem to attract more fish.

With all this in mind, ask the local tackle dealer what works best in his area. Buy that size, but try other sizes if you have them.

BAITS

Minnows are small fish that almost every big fish wants for dinner. Hooked through the lips and weighted with a sinker about 15 inches up the line they can be cast and retrieved like a lure or drifted through fish-holding water. Trout. bass and walleye like them, but pike and pickerel love them.

Crayfish are freshwater crustaceans that look like tiny lobsters. Hooked through the tail and weighted with a sinker 15 inches up the line they can be drifted and "worked" through fish-holding

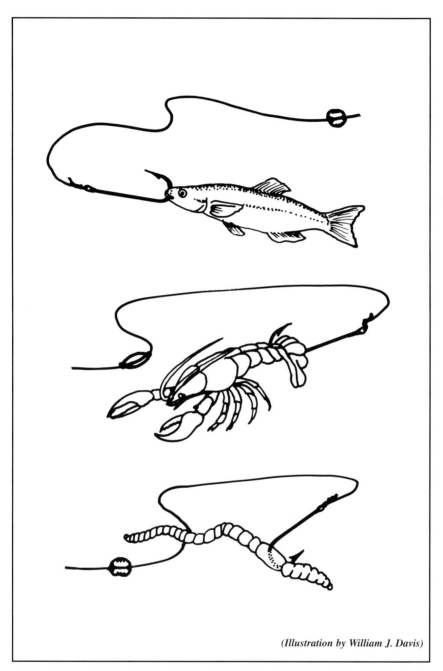

(Illustration by William J. Davis)

THE BEST BAIT RIGS FOR FISHING RIVERS AND STREAMS:
Top—a minnow hooked through the lips.
Center—a crayfish hooked through the tail.
Bottom—a worm hooked through the breeding ring.

water. Most fish eat them but trout, especially brown trout, and smallmouth bass love them.

Worms are nightcrawlers and garden worms that provide a fish buffet when washed into streams and rivers. Hooked through the breeding ring and weighted with a sinker 15 inches up the line they can be drifted through fish-holding water. Except for pike and pickerel most fish like them, but trout, walleye, fallfish and carp love them.

Note: Sinker weight is critical when fishing live bait. Use just enough weight to get the bait to the fish. For instance when fishing bait for trout in shallow runs, the weight of the hook and bait is often enough. When fishing slow and deep for walleyes, a heavy sinker is required to keep the bait on the bottom.

ACCESSORIES

TACKLE BOX OR VEST
A small plastic tackle box is ideal for canoe-fishing. It can hold terminal tackle, lures, tools and spare spools of fishing line. A fishing vest can hold all of the above and stays with you when you leave the canoe to wade or bank fish. I use both, depending on the stream. If it's a slow moving, deep water stream where I don't expect to wade, the tackle box is my choice. If it's trout or bass water consisting of a series of riffles and pools that I will surely fish on foot, the vest is best. Some streams offer both kinds of water, so both the vest and tackle box go in the canoe.

NET
A medium size landing net with a two-foot handle can save fish and fingers. Most small fish can be landed by hand, but a landing net can keep you from losing a big fish, help you release fish unharmed and keep your fingers away from sharp hooks and teeth ... at the end of a thrashing fish.

PLIERS OR FORCEPS
A pair of long nose pliers or forceps can save time, lures, fish and fingers. They are nice to have for trout and bass, and a must-have for pike, pickerel and walleye.

LINE CLIPPER

Monofilament fishing line is tough stuff, so a line clipper—looks like a finger nail clipper—can save time and teeth.

FILE OR STONE

Dull hooks don't catch fish, sharp hooks do, so a small file or hook sharpening stone should be in every tackle box.

MINNOW BUCKET

A metal or plastic minnow bucket that floats is best for canoe-fishing. You can put it over the side when time and water conditions permit. Fresh water keeps minnows alive and lively.
Crayfish can also be kept in a minnow bucket.

WORM KEEPERS

Worms like to be cool and damp. Commercial worm bedding in an aerated worm box does the trick in most situations. The styrofoam containers that bait dealers sell worms in keep them in good shape if kept cool and shaded. The best place to keep them while canoe-fishing is in a cooler. The best place at home is in the refrigerator.

NICE TO HAVE STUFF

THERMOMETER

Water temperatures determine when and which fish are most active (see Chapter 5, Fish Species), so a water thermometer can help put you into fish.

ELECTRONIC FISH FINDER

Most canoe-fishing waters are not deep enough to use a sonar device (fish finder), but in some rivers deep holes can hold concentrations of bass, trout and walleyes, or a few big fish. Finding such fish havens and knowing where the fish are (suspended or near the bottom) can lead to some exciting fishing. There are a number of portable units on the market that are perfect for canoe-fishing.

The brook trout (top) is the official state fish and our only native stream trout. The brown trout (bottom left) came to New York from Europe and is our most abundant stream trout. The rainbow trout (bottom right) came from the west coast and can tolerate warmer water than any other trout. Trout are one of the few stream fish that have an adipose fin. The easiest way to tell one trout from the other is by their spots and colors.

CHAPTER 5

FISH YOU CAN CATCH FROM A CANOE

Hundreds of species of fish live or spawn in the rivers and streams of New York State. Most are native species, but some came to our waters in wagons, ships and tanker trucks from other parts of the country and from around the world. While the study of all these fish can be fascinating, it is beyond the scope of this book. Here we will focus on ten "sport" fish you are most likely to catch while canoe-fishing New York's rivers and streams.

Knowing something about these fish can add much to your canoe-fishing experience. Such knowledge can improve your chances of catching fish and open the door to some fascinating observations. Recognizing preferred habitat, temperatures and food can help you to choose the time and place to present lure or bait. Spawning habits can point the way to concentrations of fish for observation, or when legal, for some exceptional fishing experiences.

Learning to identify the species of fish you catch from rivers and streams is not difficult and can be part of the fun. It can also keep you out of trouble. More than one stringer of "trout" caught by novice fishermen were in fact smallmouth bass taken long before the season opened. And, nothing is so remembered by family and friends as a frying pan of succulent "brookies" that are really tasteless and bony fallfish.

The following brief descriptions and tips on how to identify similar species are provided to help you catch more fish and identify what you catch. While positive identification of some species may require counting fin rays, rows of teeth or barbels, you can identify most stream fish by **knowing one or two features.**

It also helps to know the size of the fish you can expect to catch. Most of the fish that inhabit rivers and streams are not monsters,

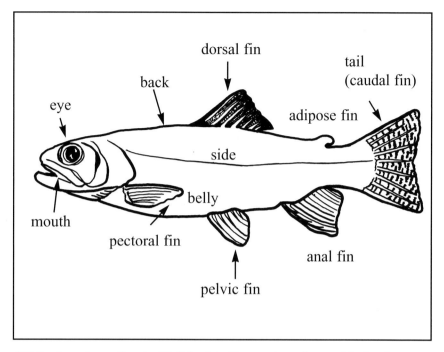

While there is no "typical" fish, this illustration along with the descriptions and photographs featured in this chapter and throughout this book, will help you to recognize the features that distinguish one species from another—and perhaps keep you out of trouble.

although some "legendary" fish are caught every year. The average stream fish works hard for it's dinner, so it never reaches the size of it's cousins who enjoy the good life of lots of food and quiet water in lakes and ocean. However, what stream fish lack in size they make up for in wariness and tenacity. That's why many anglers consider an 18-inch brown trout caught from a stream a trophy, and the same size brown taken from a lake a throwback.

TROUT
Trout have a small dorsal fin (adipose fin) just ahead of the tail, **no** barbels around the mouth, tiny soft scales, and spots on the darker colored parts of their body. Most of the spots are black or brown, but the more striking spots feature such colors as red, orange and blue.

1. BROOK TROUT
New York's official state fish and only native stream trout prefers

clean, cold, well oxygenated water and inhabits many of our mountain streams and rivers. Stocked in coldwater streams throughout the state. Preferred temperatures are 57–61 degrees F. **Spawns in the fall**, October - December, in small streams (creeks) with a good gravel bottom. Preferred foods are insects (larva and adult) small fish, and worms that wash into streams.

Brook trout feature **red spots surrounded by a blue ring, and orange to pink lower fins.** Size 9–10 inches, up to 14 inches; under 2-pounds.

2. BROWN TROUT

Came to New York from Europe in 1883. Prefers clean, moderately flowing water. Tolerates warmer water and more pollution than brook trout. Stocked in rivers and streams throughout the state. Most widely distributed trout; found in every New York State watershed. Preferred temperatures 54–64 degrees F. **Spawns in the fall**, October-November, in streams with good gravel bottom. Preferred foods are insects (larva and adult), crayfish, small fish and worms that wash into streams.

Brown trout feature **large orange and red spots, and a creamy white belly**. Size 10–12 inches, up to 20 inches; 3–4 pounds.

3. RAINBOW TROUT

Came to New York from the west coast in 1874. Prefers fast-flowing, turbulent streams. Can tolerate water temperatures up to 80 degrees F.,higher than any other New York trout. Stocked in many rivers and streams throughout the state. Preferred temperatures 57 –60 degrees F. **Spawns in the spring**, March - April, in streams with good gravel bottom. Preferred foods are insects (larva and adult) fish eggs and small fish.

Rainbow trout feature **many small dark spots, pink to red "rainbow" sides, and a white to silver belly**. Size 10–12 inches, up to 18 inches, 2-pounds.

BASS

Bass are of the sunfish family, but are longer and larger than most of their cousins. Like all sunfish they have a spiny dorsal fin and hard scales.

Northern pike (right) have a long body, dorsal and anal fins near the tail, duckbill toothy jaws and light bean-shaped spots on its sides. It's cousin, the chain pickerel (below) has the same body, fins and jaws but has "chain-like" markings on its sides.

Walleye (left) have canine teeth, two dorsal fins and a white tip on the tail. Smallmouth bass (right) are identified by their body shape, side markings and by the fact that the back corner of the mouth is even with the eye.

4. SMALLMOUTH BASS

A native fish that reproduces naturally in most New York rivers and streams. Prefers moderate to fast water near rocks. Preferred temperatures 65–75 degrees F. **Spawns in spring**, May-June, over gravel or rocky bottom. Preferred foods are insects (larva and adult), crayfish and small fish.

Smallmouth bass are brown to greenish brown and often feature **vertical bars on sides. Back corner of the mouth is even with the eye**. Size 10–14 inches, up to 18 inches; 3-pounds.

*Note: Largemouth bass are not common in New York streams, preferring the calm weedy waters of ponds and lakes. However, they are occasionally caught by stream anglers, usually in large river bays and near the inlets and outlets of lakes and ponds. The largemouth bass has a green to black body with a **dark horizontal band on sides** from head to tail. **Back corner of the mouth extends behind the eye**—hence "largemouth".*

5. ROCK BASS

A husky sunfish that is found in the same water as smallmouth bass. Preferred temperatures 60–70 degrees F. **Spawns in early summer**. Preferred foods are insects (larva and adult) crayfish, small fish, and worms that wash into streams. When the smallmouths won't bite, rock bass can save the day.

Rock bass are dark olive in color with **dark splotches on sides. Eyes are red**. Size 7–9 inches, up to 12 inches, 1-pound.

PIKE

Pike are elongated fish with dorsal and anal fins located near the tail. Duckbill jaws have large pointed and very sharp teeth. Very slimy to touch.

6. NORTHERN PIKE

A native fish that reproduces naturally in many New York rivers and streams. Prefers slow to still water in or near weeds. Preferred temperatures 50–70 degrees F. **Spawns in spring just after ice out** in shallow marshes and flooded meadows. Preferred foods are other fish, but will also eat crayfish, frogs and ducklings.

Northern pike are dark to greenish brown with **light bean-**

shaped spots on sides, and a white belly. Size 20–30 inches, up to 36 inches, 10-pounds.

7. CHAIN PICKEREL
A native fish that reproduces naturally in some New York streams. Prefers slow to still water in weeds. Preferred temperatures 50–70 degrees F. **Spawns in spring just after ice out** in shallow bays and marshes. Preferred foods are other fish.

Chain Pickerel are green to brown with **black "chain"-like markings on sides.** Size 14–16 inches, up to 18 inches; 3-pounds.

Note: Muskellunge are not common in New York rivers and streams but they are occasionally caught by stream anglers. Muskies are green, gold to light brown with **dark vertical bars on sides, and a cream belly.** Tiger Muskies—a cross between a northern pike and muskellunge—have **dark vertical bars on sides with "electric blue" background coloration.**

8. WALLEYE
A native fish that reproduces naturally in many New York rivers and streams. Prefers moderate-flowing, clean but cloudy water with sand and gravel bottom. Preferred temperatures 60–70 degrees. **Spawns in spring** on gravel bottom soon after ice-out and water temperatures are 45–50 F. Preferred foods are fish, crayfish, insect larva and worms that wash into streams.

Walleye are grayish yellow to brownish (golden) yellow with dark bands or blotches on sides. Has **two dorsal fins and a forked tail that is white on the lower lobe.** Canine teeth in lower jaw, and large "glassy" eyes. Size: 15–18 inches, up to 20 inches; 3-pounds.

"SPORT" MINNOWS
Two large "minnows" contribute significantly to the fun of canoe-fishing by providing "action" when other fish have lockjaw.

9. FALLFISH
New York's largest native freshwater minnow inhabits most New York rivers and streams. Prefers moderate to slow water with gravel to rocky bottom. Preferred temperatures are unknown, but are active from late spring to early fall. **Spawns in May on huge nests**

When other fish have lockjaw, these three fish often save the day. Fallfish (top) are found in the same stream as trout and bass. There is no mistaking its silvery sides and single dorsal fin. Rock bass (bottom left) are found in the same waters as smallmouth bass. There is no mistaking its red eye, body shape and markings. Carp (bottom right) are found in most New York watersheds and grow to huge size. There is no mistaking its large hard scales and the barbels on its mouth.

that the male fallfish builds by carrying rocks and pebbles in its mouth and piling them in mounds as large as six feet long and three feet high. Preferred foods are insects (larva and adult) crayfish, small fish and worms that wash into streams. Fallfish can save the day when trout and bass are not active.

Fallfish have an **olive brown back, silvery sides, barbels on its mouth, but does not have an adipose fin**.
Size: 10–15 inches, up to 18 inches; 2-pounds.

10. CARP

New York's largest freshwater minnow came to New York from Europe by ship in the 1830's, and are now living and spawning in most streams and rivers. Prefers moderate to still water with weeds and muddy bottom. Tolerates pollution, high temperatures and low oxygen levels. Preferred temperatures 60–90 degrees F. **Spawns — with much splashing—in spring**, May and June, in weedy shallows. Preferred foods are insect larva,. mollusks, worms and almost anything edible they can suck into their mouth.

Carp are **brownish yellow with large hard scales, long dorsal fin and four barbels on its mouth**. Size: 18–20 inches, up to 24 inches; 10-pounds.

OTHER FISH

There are a variety of other fish caught by stream fishermen, but are seldom caught by canoe-fishermen. For instance bullheads are abundant in New York rivers and streams but are usually caught by anglers who fish in one place for hours.

Ocean and lake fish enter our rivers and streams during the spawning run, but they are not generally caught by canoe-fishermen because of season restrictions, waters that are too rough and cold to canoe safely, concentrations of boat or bank fishermen, and relatively short spawning periods. Fish that fall in this category are striped bass, shad, chinook salmon, coho salmon, landlocked salmon, rainbow trout and steelhead.

Waters where some of these fish were taken by canoe-fishermen are covered in Section Two.

CHAPTER 6

HOW TO FISH
FROM A CANOE

Fishing from a canoe is anything but boring. How you do it depends on the type of stream, the species of fish, whether you fish with bait or lures ... and your mood at the time. Quite simply, you have to put your offerings where the fish are and not spook them. If you're a stream fisherman, the transition is easy because you know where the fish are and what they want to eat.

Fishing from a moving canoe, however, is not the same as fishing from a stationary position. Generally, the canoe—and you—move downstream faster than the lure or bait, so you have to cast diagonally downstream, or ahead of the canoe, to allow your offering to sink before you work it through fishy water.

It's great fun to cast to pools, pockets and other fish havens as you zip by in the canoe. This is also a good way to quickly locate hungry fish—and lose lures if your casting skills are not up to par. I like the feel of the canoe, to see the river, to find out what's around the next bend, so that's how I do most of my canoe-fishing. But, to really do it right, to fish a stream thoroughly, to catch wary, slow moving, or sluggish fish, it's best to fish from a stationary or slow moving canoe, or if possible, by wading the stream. In some areas the stream offers still or slow-moving water within casting distance of fish havens, so you can easily fish from the canoe. Where that's not possible, tying or anchoring the canoe, or going on foot, is the way to catch fish.

A neat trick I learned from Adirondack guide, Joe Hackett is to secure 10-foot lengths of rope near or to the bow and stern seats. They allow one or both anglers to tie the canoe to streamside brush and branches within casting distance of fish cover.

By anchoring above or to the side of prime water and letting the canoe "hang" in the current, you can effectively fish the best runs, holes and obstructions.

A WORD OF CAUTION: *Don't anchor a canoe in fast, rough water unless you are prepared to get wet. It will flip over.*

If a stretch of stream looks especially good, pass it by, beach the canoe and fish upstream on foot. In some areas, especially in shallow, narrow streams where the canoe must pass over fish, it's best to beach the canoe upstream and walk the bank downstream to fish productive waters.

Always try to stay away from fish-holding waters with the canoe. That big shadow can really spook fish, especially in shallow water. Noise can do the same, so lower the anchor, don't toss it, and be careful moving tackle boxes and other gear in the bottom of the canoe.

WHEN THE CURRENT IS MOVING FASTER THAN YOU

When the current is moving faster than you are, cast diagonally upstream and slightly beyond where fish are holding. This allows the lure or bait time to sink before you work it by the fish's nose. In slower moving water the same presentation takes fish, however, you also have the options of casting cross stream, downstream and directly upstream, depending on water depth and speed, and weight of lure or bait.

LURES

More stream fish are caught on spinners than any other lure, because they are easier to fish than any other lure. Yet, some stream anglers catch more and bigger fish on plugs, spoons, jigs **and** spinners simply because they know how they work and how to work them.

Lures are supposed to look like food to feeding fish. (See Chapter 4) A lure that looks more like natural food, or better yet, natural food in trouble, catches fish.

Spinners, depending on their design, flash and vibrate through the water like a minnow on the run, so even a straight retrieve can turn on a hungry fish. A spoon on the other hand requires more finesse, so rod tip action and changes in reel speed to make the spoon look like a wounded minnow are more effective. Sometimes spinners are more effective using these same techniques.

Plugs, depending on their design, also represent fish food. The Rapala minnow looks more like a swimming minnow if the recommended loop knot is used to tie it to fishing line. It looks more like a wounded minnow if the rod tip is twitched from time to time.

The Rebel Crawfish looks like a crayfish trying to get away. It looks more like a crayfish if it nudges the bottom from time to time. If the short-lipped version doesn't reach the bottom, try the big-lipped deep divers.

Jigs look like a variety of fish foods, so a variety of retrieves are in order. Just swimming the jig with a few changes in reel speed can take fish. Jerking the rod tip up, retrieving slack line and then jerking again turns some fish on. Sometimes a slow lift instead of the jerk upward works best.

Spinner-jigs work well on a straight retrieve, but are sometimes most effective sinking towards the bottom, so a let-sink, slow-lift retrieve works best.

Don't be afraid to experiment with changes in lures, lure speed and rod tip action.

Some situations require special skills and techniques to present lures to feeding fish. For example a fish haven the size of a small bathtub, requires pin point accuracy and an immediate retrieve to get results. Getting a lure to the fish in a pile of logs or undercut bank, may require allowing the lure to drift downstream into this type of cover before retrieving it—much like fishing bait.

BAIT

Worms, minnows and crayfish are the most popular baits. (See Chapter 4.)

Hook a worm or nightcrawler (sometimes half a nightcrawler is plenty) through the middle or the breeding ring. Cast it above fish havens and let it sink to the bottom. Take in slack line, leaving a good bend, and allow the bait to drift downstream. When you feel a hit or see the line tighten or jump, set the hook. Remember, use just enough sinker to take the bait to the bottom. A Size-6 hook is good for most situations, but a Size-8 or 10 will often take more fish in clear water.

Hook a minnow up through the lips and fish it like a worm, or retrieve it with a slow twitching motion of the rod tip. In deeper, slow-moving water a minnow can be hooked through the back just ahead of the dorsal fin and fished below a bobber. This is especially effective for northern pike and pickerel. Hook size depends on the size of the minnow and fish you expect to catch. Number 8 or 6 is good for the smaller trout and bass minnows, and Number 4 or larger for pike minnows.

Hook a crayfish up through the tail, about three segments from the tip. After drifting the crayfish through fishy water, let it swing around in the current. Get ready for a hit. If you don't get a hit and the water is deep enough, work the bait toward you with a slow jerking motion. A Size-4 hook will do fine.

As with lures, presenting bait is not always as simple as casting, drifting and retrieving. Sometimes special techniques are required for special places. Some situations require hand-feeding the line as the bait drifts directly downstream into a hole or pool. When the bottom is so cluttered with rubble that it "eats" tackle, bait suspended from a small bobber or a float will take fish.

WHERE THEY ARE AND WHAT THEY LIKE
A number of species of fish can live in the same stream. Yet they prefer different habitats, different food ... and different lures and bait. The following information along with that provided in Chapter 5 can help you find and catch more fish.

TROUT
Trout are the most sought after stream fish in New York State. Brown trout are the most abundant because they tolerate a wide range of water quality and temperatures, so most of our trout streams are well stocked with browns. Brook trout like cold to cool water year round so they are usually found in mountain or spring-fed streams. Rainbow trout are also stocked in many New York streams because they can tolerate relatively high water temperatures. Unfortunately, rainbows don't stick around. If possible, they eventually move downstream to bigger waters.

Except for rainbows, trout stay out of rapids, preferring instead to hold just out of fast water where meals are delivered by the cur-

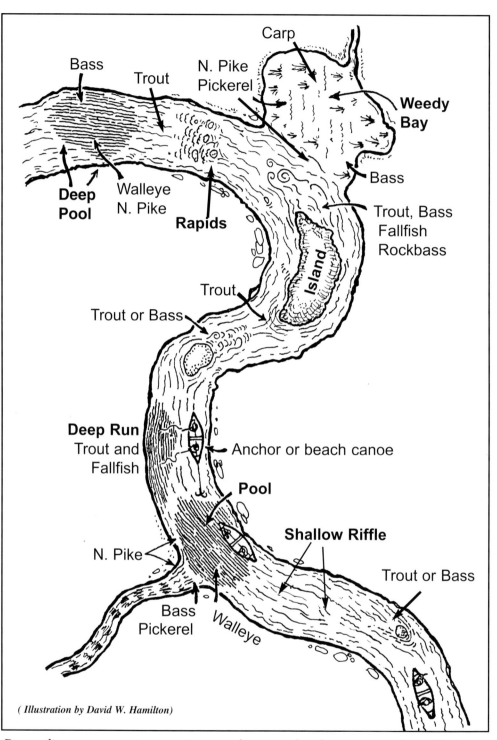

Depending on water temperatures and oxygen levels many species of fish can live in the same stream, however, they usually prefer different habitats and different food. Knowing where and how to present a lure or bait, and how to avoid spooking fish, can help to insure success.

rent and minimum energy is required to stay in feeding position. Trout wait for food at the head and tail of pools, near islands, rocks, logs, bridge abutments, undercut banks and in long deep runs. Those slow-water pools below islands, large rocks and bridge abutments provide trout havens that can extend downstream for 50 yards or more.

During the summer months, anything that can offer cool water, oxygen and shade will attract trout, so coldwater springs, stream outlets, pools below rapids, riffles and waterfalls, and shoreline shade will concentrate fish.

Trout like spinners, spoons and plugs and small jigs that look like minnows, crayfish and insects. The best bait for brown and brook trout is a worm, with minnows and crayfish running a close second. Rainbow trout prefer minnows but will take worms.

SMALLMOUTH BASS
Smallmouths are the most abundant sportfish in New York streams. They like clear, cool, moving water, but can tolerate a wide range of stream conditions. They especially like pools and eddies below rapids and waterfalls, small bays, quiet water at stream bends, rock piles, logs, stream outlets, islands and bridge abutments. In shallow water streams one to two fish will hold in small pockets near rocks, logs and other obstructions. In big rivers smallmouths will school up.

Smallmouths like spinners, plugs, jigs and spinner-jigs that look like minnows, crayfish and insects. The best bait for smallies is a crayfish. Second best is a minnow.

ROCKBASS
Rockbass hold in the same water and take the same lures and bait as smallmouth bass. They will also take small jigs suspended from a bobber. They love worms.

NORTHERN PIKE
There are more northern pike in New York rivers and streams than most people realize. If there are deep pools, weeds in the river and access to weedy bays and/or flooded meadows (for spawning),

northern pike can set up housekeeping.

Many slow-moving, weed-infested streams are noted pike waters. Not so well-known are some trout streams that hold big stream pike. More than once I've been skunked at a "trout" pool until a big minnow enticed the resident northern pike that ruled that roost.

Northerns take their stations in deep pools, weedy bays and near log piles and stream outlets.

Flashy spinners and spoons are the best lures. Minnows are far and away the best bait. Generally, big pike like big lures and big minnows.

CHAIN PICKEREL

Chain Pickerel prefer slow-moving weedy streams, or streams that offer access to weedy bays or tributaries. The best places to fish for them are in open pockets in the weeds or at the edge of the weeds (the weedline).

They like the same lures and bait as northern pike.

WALLEYE

Walleye are a very popular stream fish during spawning runs, but when they return to their resident lakes and rivers, most fishermen look elsewhere for walleye. That's a shame because many New York rivers and streams hold walleye all year long.

Walleye prefer the bottom of deep pools at bends in the river, near piles of logs, tree roots, rocks, bridge abutments and stream outlets. In the evening and on cloudy days they often move out of the deep pools to feed near piles of debris and along the weedline.

They like jigs, spinners and plugs that look like insect larva, leeches and minnows. The best bait is a nightcrawler. Second best is a minnow.

Slow-moving lures and baits on the bottom work best.

FALLFISH

Most fallfish are caught by anglers seeking trout and bass, because they inhabit the same waters and hit many of the same lures and bait.

Bob McNitt took this 5-pound northern pike from the upper reaches of Chenango River by beaching the canoe well upstream and walking the bank downstream to effectively fish one of his favorite "trout" pools.

Sometimes the best way to reach fish with lure or bait is to anchor the canoe upstream or to one side of productive waters.

Fallfish like the quiet waters of pools, holes, eddies and small bays, but will feed in fast water where they can stay out of the current behind rocks or other obstructions.

They like flashy spoons and spinners. They love worms.

CARP

Carp are despised by most stream fishermen—until they catch one on light tackle.

Carp like mud and weeds. During the summer months carp will lay in water so shallow their backs are out of the water.

They like jigs. They love worms.

CHAPTER 7

WILDLIFE YOU CAN SEE FROM A CANOE

Every waterway in New York, no matter how wild or urban, is home to an amazing variety of wildlife. Some of these wild creatures live in or near free-flowing water all their lives; some breed, raise their young and depart as soon as they can travel; others stay until ice-over, and a few merely stop to rest and feed. While in-depth Field Guides to birds and mammals are required to recognize all of these many species, the following brief descriptions will help to identify 10 of the most common birds and animals you are likely to see while canoe-fishing New York rivers and streams. Others are listed at the end of the chapter.

1. GREAT BLUE HERON

Once a rare sight in New York, the great blue heron is found on every river and stream in the state during all seasons except late winter. The great blue is our largest bird with a wingspan of up to six feet. Standing on long legs, it's three feet tall. Upper body is dark grey, lower body light grey, head white with a black crest, and wings a dark grey-blue with black shoulders. Females and males look the same. Wades in shallow water to catch fish with its long beak. When not wading, stands on logs and rocks, or perches in streamside trees. Flies ahead of canoe, often squawks displeasure.

2. COMMON MERGANSER

One of the largest ducks and the most abundant waterfowl on New York rivers and streams from ice-out to ice-over. Both the mature male and female have light underbodies and wings, but their similarity during the spring breeding season ends there. Female and immature birds have silver-grey backs and sides with tufted reddish-brown heads. Mature males have dark green heads (which usually

Canoe-fishing offers unique opportunities to see and photograph wildlife. This seemingly passive pair of mute swans on the Delaware River attacked the anglers in the red canoe when they accidently got too close to their nest.

This young whitetail deer entertained us for 10 minutes on Rondout Creek

look black) and black and white bodies. After molting in mid summer and well into fall, males look like females.

They dive to catch fish (and crayfish) with long bills that have saw-like teeth. When not feeding, mergansers sit low in the water or rest on rocks, logs or gravel and sand bars. Seem to run across the water when taking off. Fly ahead of the canoe, returning upstream during the spring nesting season. Young birds and molting adults will often "run" on the water, creating a water-spraying spectacle. In the fall mergansers "herd" downstream ahead of the canoe, forming large flocks. Calls are low, short quacks.

3. MALLARD

The most common and one of the largest ducks in New York. Abundant on rivers and streams during the spring nesting season, much less so in late summer and fall when young require less cover and can fly to better food sources. Both male and female have off-white under wings and a blue bar with white border (speculum) on top of wings. Female is mottled brown. Male has a green head, white neck band, chestnut breast and grey body. Males and females look alike after molting in June and well into September.

Adults and young feed on insects and crustaceans in spring; seeds and plants as the season progresses, and on domestic grains in the fall. When not feeding, mallards sit high on the water or rest on rocks, logs or along shoreline. Adults literally jump off the water when disturbed, flying downstream from the canoe and almost always circling back upstream. Hens with young seek shoreline cover. Calls are a variety of loud quacks.

4. WOOD DUCK

A smaller duck and not as abundant as the merganser and mallard on New York rivers and streams. However, they are almost always seen on woodland streams where they nest in hollows in trees. The female has a white belly, light underwings and grey-brown wings with blue bars (speculum). Her body is grey-brown with white dashes on the sides. With a dark crested head, white chin and throat, and white ring around the eye, she is one of the more striking female ducks.

The male wood duck is the most beautiful duck in New York, perhaps in the world, with red eyes and red base of his bill; a crested head colored in many shades of green and purple accented by white lines; a burgundy chest, flecked with white; a white belly and mottled beige sides, iridescent purple wings with blue bars, and a purple and green tail. After molting in the summer, males look much like females and immature birds until mid October when their colorful plumage returns.

Adults and young feed on insects early in the spring and then switch to vegetation, with acorns being a favorite repast. Wood ducks sit high on the water and often rest on logs and in trees. Like the mallard they jump off the water, flying downstream and circling back when disturbed. Hens and young seek shoreline cover. The female's loud squealing call or whistle is very distinctive and usually heard before she is seen.

5. CANADA GOOSE

A decade ago Canada geese on New York rivers and streams were an uncommon sight except during migration periods, and then only on larger waters. Today, Canadas nest and raise their young on streams throughout the state, and remain in the area as long as food and open water are available.

The distinctive long black neck, black head and white cheek, broad wings and large body make the Canada easy to identify. Back and wings are grey-brown to dark brown, lower body is grey, shading to a white belly. Females and males look identical throughout the year. Generally, a Canada goose is much larger than a mallard, although some smaller, mallard-size Canadas are seen on rivers and streams in New York.

Canadas are more often seen on smaller streams during the spring when breeding pairs nest and raise their young. When disturbed they run across the water to take flight downstream and then circle back to nesting sites. With young, they swim to shore and run to cover. Later in the year, flocks of Canadas are found on larger rivers. Canadas nest and congregate close to grain fields whenever possible. There is no mistaking their honking call—or V formations when flying overhead.

6. OSPREY

Once rare, the osprey or "fish hawk" is frequently seen on New York rivers and streams where it nests and feeds. Easily recognized by its large size, crooked wing (wingspan 4 1/2 feet), white head, white underbody and underwings, and dark grey-brown upper body and wings. **A big hawk, white on bottom, dark on top is almost always an osprey.** Females and males look the same.

Osprey nest and rest high in dead trees. Often seen diving to catch fish holding or swimming near the surface, and then carrying it in its talons to a tree for dinner. Call is a series of loud, clear whistles.

7. KINGFISHER

This big-headed, short-tailed bird that looks like a large blue jay is quite common on rivers and streams throughout New York. Its crested head, upper body, breast band and wings are blue-grey; neck and belly are white. Females have a bright chestnut band across the belly.

A Kingfisher dives into streams to catch small fish with their large pointed beak. Also eat crayfish and frogs. They perch in trees over water and fly upstream or down when disturbed, usually scolding intruders with a loud rattling call.

8. MUSKRAT

The most common mammal seen on rivers and streams in New York is the muskrat. It's thick set, dark-brown body is sometimes mistaken for a small beaver, but it's long, round tail, in no way compares with the broad, flat beaver tail. Muskrats breed, eat and live year round on and near the water. They build dome-shaped homes of cattails and other vegetation in marshes, but make their streamside homes in burrows in stream banks. They feed on marsh and streamside vegetation.

In the water at a distance a muskrat looks like a head with a wake, but up close the body and tail "rudder" are clearly visible. When approached they usually dive, sometimes swimming right under the canoe.

9. BEAVER

Once almost extinct in New York, the beaver is now found on most rivers and streams, and is in fact the official state mammal. It's dark, large body (almost 3-feet long and weighing 40–60 pounds when full grown), rounded head and broad, flat tail are easy to recognize.

Beaver breed, eat and live year-round on and near the water. They use tree branches and mud to build large domed houses and dams, but will also burrow into streambanks to make dens. They feed on grasses, cattails and other water plants early in the summer, but switch to buds and bark of trees in the fall and winter. In some areas beaver have developed a taste for corn stalks.

Canoe-fishermen see more beaver sign than they do the animal itself. Beaver tracks in the mud, beaver slides down streambanks, piles of branches and cornstalks at the water's edge, beaver houses, beaver dams and chewed trees, are all evidence of a healthy beaver population. However, seeing a beaver out of water is a rare sight, because they disappear very quickly when anything out of the ordinary moves into the area. Unless prepared to wait and watch, the closest most canoe-fishermen come to seeing and hearing a beaver is: watching a green leafy branch moving cross stream with a wake behind it, and hearing the "whack" of its tale slapping water as it dives out of sight.

10. WHITETAIL DEER

Whitetail deer are very common along rivers and streams throughout the state. An average deer is 3-feet tall at the shoulder, 6-feet long and weighs 140 pounds. Colors are tan to reddish brown in the spring and summer; brown to grey in the fall and winter). Considering its size, color, big ears and white tail, it should be easy to see from a canoe. Not so, because most deer move to cover when they see, hear or smell what doesn't fit in their environment. So, most canoe-fishermen see lots and lots of deer tracks in the mud and sand, and well-traveled deer trails leading to river banks, but they seldom see a deer.

Whitetails are seen more often in the spring and fall because there is less cover than during the summer. Hugging inside turns in a stream and keeping noise to a minimum improves the chances of seeing deer --- not always easy when fishing from a canoe, but well worth doing when approaching recognized deer crossings and feeding areas.

OTHER WILDLIFE

There are many more species of wildlife that live near or visit rivers and streams in New York. Canoe-fishermen have a very good chance of seeing the following: Green Heron, Red-tailed Hawk, Great Horned Owl, Turkey Vulture, Crow, Raven, Ruffed Grouse, Wild Turkey, Mute Swan, Killdeer, Sandpiper, Raccoon, Woodchuck, River Otter, Fox, Coyote, Grey Squirrel, several species of turtles and snakes, and an amazing variety of song-birds.

The following Field Guides offer excellent descriptions and color photographs of many of these species. They are available in book stores.

Birds of the Adirondacks

Mammals of the Adirondacks

The Audubon Society Field Guide to Mammals

The Audubon Society Field Guide to Birds - Eastern Region

A Guide to Field Identification - Birds of North America

Peterson Field Guides - Eastern Birds

CHAPTER 8

HOW TO PLAN A CANOE-FISHING TRIP

Assuming you have the knowledge, skills and equipment discussed in previous chapters, you can plan a successful canoe-fishing trip —with these basic ingredients: a stream that offers reasonably good fishing, easywater that's deep enough to canoe, places to put the canoe in and take it out, knowledge of major obstructions, and judgment in deciding the practical length of the trip.

GOOD FISHING STREAMS

The second half of this book highlights 25 of the better New York canoe-fishing rivers and streams, but there are hundreds, perhaps thousands of miles of similar streams throughout the state. Some of them offer miles and miles of uninterrupted trips, others offer short stretches of easywater. Part of the fun is finding your secret stretch of water where the canoeing is easy and the fishing is great. Chances are that stream is very close to your backyard.

Most rivers and streams in New York offer good to excellent fishing thanks to the "Pure Waters" laws that were enacted a couple of decades ago. Enforcement of these laws have cleaned up our waters so much that the natural reproduction of many fish species has increased dramatically. In addition to this natural reproduction, the New York State Department of Environmental Conservation (DEC) stocks trout in many streams throughout the state.

WATER DEEP ENOUGH TO CANOE

Water levels are a major consideration when planning a canoe-fishing trip. May and June are the best months to canoe-fish most New York rivers and streams. The high waters of spring runoff have subsided and there is still plenty of ground water and rain-fall.

During the summer months smaller streams are generally too low to canoe-fish. This is the time to plan trips on larger waters and waters controlled by dams. Finding larger waters may mean canoeing a downstream section of the same stream you canoe-fished earlier in the year, or giving some of the larger rivers a try.

Power dams and water-control dams regulate the water in some streams and provide "high" water at certain times of day throughout the year. The trick is to know when water is released, so you can "ride" it with your canoe. This release often occurs in the morning and lasts a few hours. Keep in mind that during the release the water is "UP" close to the dam in the morning, but won't be "UP" several miles downstream until afternoon. Incidentally, rising water can turn fish on.

Information on water release times is often available at local tackle shops, campgrounds and restaurants. Some power companies have telephone "hotlines" that provide information on water releases and stream conditions.

As rainfall increases and temperatures decrease during the fall some of the smaller streams are again canoeable.

WHERE TO PUT IN AND TAKE OUT

Canoe-fishermen let the current do the work while they fish most rivers and streams, so it's downstream all the way, except to retrieve lures or to get back to a real hotspot. So, most trips require two vehicles, one to leave at the end of the stretch of stream and one to carry the canoe to the starting point. Finding areas to put a canoe in and take it out—and park a vehicle—is not always easy.

Bridges are the most obvious access points to any stream, because they are usually on public property and parking is possible nearby. Many smaller bridges have been closed in recent years, and although access to the water is possible, crossing these bridges with a vehicle is impossible. Sometimes not knowing a bridge is out can make it very difficult to set up a trip.

Other access points are: fishermen parking areas, state and local parks, community access sites, private access with permission, and in areas where the stream and highway run side by side.

Access points can change from year to year. The only way to know for sure is to scout the area. An excellent source of information on the locations of roads and bridges along even the smallest streams are county road maps and the DeLorme "New York State Atlas & Gazetteer". An excellent source of information on the location of streams is the "New York Stream Map and Location Guide", and the best way to locate rapids and stream obstructions is with a topographical map of the area. See the back of this book for information on where to buy these publications.

MAJOR OBSTRUCTIONS

It's a good idea to start canoe-fishing on a stream that you know so there are few surprises—like rapids, falls, dams and long stretches of stillwater. If the stream is unfamiliar, check it out by driving near it, fishing it from shore, by studying topographical or county maps, or by talking to local fishermen or canoeists. There are a number of sources of information about canoe-fishing and canoeing in New York. Some of them are listed in the back of this book.

Rapids and falls are obvious dangers, but long stretches of stillwater can really mess up a canoe-fishing trip by adding hours of paddling and extending your time on the river well into the night. Years ago my canoe-fishing partner had to hitchhike to our downstream vehicle because we didn't properly scout the river. We knew there was a dam downstream, but didn't know it backed up seven miles of river, creating a stillwater that would take hours to paddle. Throughout the day we fished for trout in fast to moderate flowing water, so we expected to cover the entire stretch long before dark. Fortunately, just before dark we reached a stretch of the stillwater that ran along a highway.

HOW LONG A TRIP IS PRACTICAL

The stillwater incident illustrates that planning the length of a canoe-fishing trip is not as cut and dry as it may seem. In addition to obstructions and the rate of current flow, the length of the stream and how well you plan to fish it, have to be considered.

Many novice canoe-fishermen don't realize that the length of the water is much longer than the length of the road between two points on a stream. Most streams anyway.

If you plan to zip right along, casting to likely looking waters and stopping occasionally, you can cover a lot of water in a few hours. If on the other hand, you take the time to fish every riffle and hole, nook and cranny, hours go by but miles do not.

A six-mile trip can take up to five hours depending on how fast

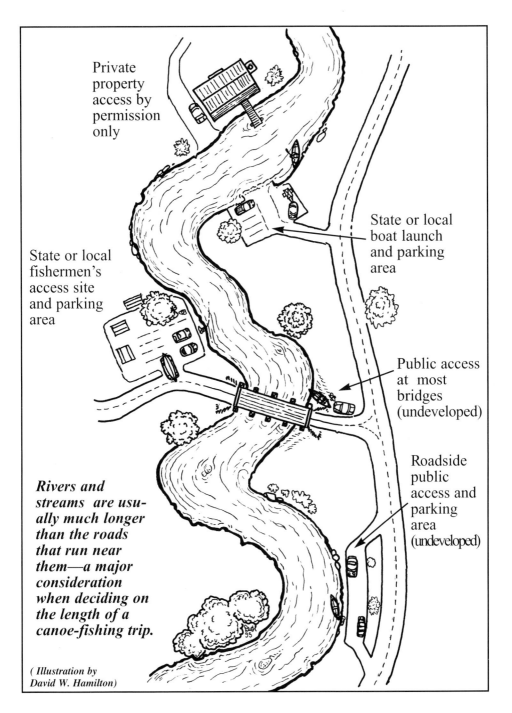

Private property access by permission only

State or local boat launch and parking area

State or local fishermen's access site and parking area

Public access at most bridges (undeveloped)

Roadside public access and parking area (undeveloped)

Rivers and streams are usually much longer than the roads that run near them—a major consideration when deciding on the length of a canoe-fishing trip.

(*Illustration by David W. Hamilton*)

To plan a successful canoe-fishing trip you need to decide on the length of the trip and locate put-in and take-out sites where you can park upstream and downstream vehicles. In most areas fishing access sites, boat launches, roadside parking areas and bridges are the best places to find access to the water.

the current is and how much you fish. Until I get to know a river, six miles is plenty for me for a day of canoe-fishing. But, when I know where the hotspots are and how fast I can travel, I'll try longer stretches.

CAMPING

Camping on a river or stream can extend canoe-fishing time considerably, but it also presents a new set of planning problems. Campsites for one. On many streams there are informal sites where you can set up camp without difficulty, however, in some areas, camping is restricted to public lands, private lands with permission, or banned altogether. You need to know if campsites are available before you start a trip.

Unless you have specific information from the New York State Department of Environmental Conservation, county or town officials, or private landowners, a scouting trip is necessary to find areas you can camp.

25 RIVERS AND STREAMS

Selecting 25 rivers and streams from the hundreds of waters that can be canoe-fished in New York State was a unique experience. I wanted to include as many streams as possible from every area of the state that would fit the criteria of free-flowing, easywater where there were fish to catch and wildlife to see. There was so little information available in most areas, I decided to canoe-fish each stream myself so the information provided would be as current and accurate as possible. Of course the prospect of canoeing, fishing and seeing wildlife on a variety of waters with kindred spirits from all over New York was very exciting and, it turned out, an opportunity of a lifetime.

In most instances I relied on the suggestions of outdoor writers, guides, DEC personnel and other friends to locate the best rivers and streams to canoe-fish throughout the state. When possible these individuals joined me on the streams in their area, adding much to the experience and the information acquired. On occasion I had to ask long time canoe-fishing friends to join me in an "adventure" on streams we knew almost nothing about. On these streams I used (and often relearned) the methods described in Chapter 8 "How To Plan A Canoe-Fishing Trip".

Generally, I selected 5–6 miles of a free-flowing stream for a day of canoe-fishing, however, both shorter and longer runs are also included. More often than not the shorter runs were determined by the time I had to spend in the area and not the stream. On some streams two or more runs were made.

I have divided this section into four chapters: Northern, Central, Southern and Western Rivers and Streams. This is a very loose delineation in some areas, however, it does help to organize this part of the book and allows the reader to locate individual streams without flipping through too many pages.

In each chapter rivers and streams are listed as I canoe-fished them, not in alphabetical order. Most of these runs took place during a threeyear period and include spring, summer and fall outings. I believe this sequence best relates the changes in the seasons, weather, water conditions, activity of wildlife and, of course, fishing throughout the year.

I discovered early on that most of the free-flowing streams are in northern and central New York, hence the preponderance of these streams. My problem in these areas was choosing which ones to include. I had to leave out some really good ones. They're listed at the end of each chapter.

Many streams originate in the Catskills and in the highlands on the east side of the Hudson River, but few of these southern waters offer enough free-flowing water for a day or even a half day of canoe-fishing. I have included most of them and noted a few others at the end of the chapter.

In the western part of the state there are only a few streams that offer free-flowing waters that are easy to canoe and hold fish, and most of them are in the southwestern part of the state. I have included most of them. I visited streams in the northwest but found them too big (Niagara River), too slow (Oak Orchard Creek) or too clogged with logs (Tonawanda) for a day of easywater canoe-fishing. These and other streams in the area do offer short stretches of excellent canoe-fishing water.

The launch and takeout points, and sometimes alternate access areas, are included in the text of each report. Other sources of information about streams, area attractions and accommodations are noted in the text or at the end of the chapter.

Each outing is related as it happened. If the fishing was lousy on a particular stream while I was there, that's how it's reported. Depending on the time of year, the weather and the mood of the fish, even the best fisherman can go fishless on some days, so I also include information on the quality of fishing as told to me by others.

If I (or we) made mistakes planning the trip or during the trip, that's how it's reported. We learn (or relearn) from our mistakes, so I have tried to emphasize them in each report. Likewise I have emphasized the things we did right or discovered that added to the adventure.

You will note that when the fishing is poor, I often provide more information about flora and fauna. That's the beauty of canoe-fishing. If the fish don't provide entertainment, then the wildlife, vegetation and the river itself does. Sometimes everything comes together—canoeing, fishing, weather, water, wildlife, trees, flowers —to provide an almost magical adventure. You'll find I have enjoyed more than my share of such magic while canoe-fishing the rivers and streams of New York.

CHAPTER 9
NORTHERN

CHAPTER 10
CENTRAL

CHAPTER 11
SOUTHERN

CHAPTER 12
WESTERN

CHAPTER 9

NORTHERN RIVERS AND STREAMS

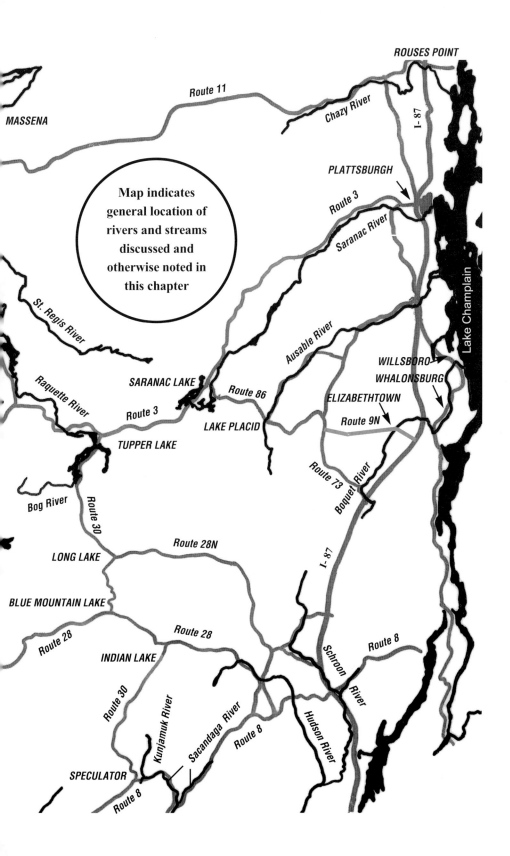

AUSABLE RIVER

The Ausable River near Lake Placid is one of the most famous trout streams in the Northeast. Anglers travel hundreds of miles to wade these Adirondack Mountain waters and cast to rising browns, rainbows and brook trout. Much of this stream is accessible from paved roads, so the trout become so educated they are almost impossible to catch on a fly or lure. Not so if you fish from a canoe.

I had waded this river a number of times over the years, and the parts I fished were boulder strewn or much too shallow or rough to fish from a canoe, so I was surprised when Joe Hackett suggested the Ausable when I asked him to guide me to some Adirondack rivers and streams that were easy to canoe-fish.

"There is a three-mile section of the West Branch of the Ausable that starts near the Lake Placid airport and runs to the bridge on Route 86 that is perfect for canoe-fishing in the spring", Joe explained. "This area is well stocked, so there are plenty of fish and the water is high enough to work with a canoe."

We could hear the announcer at a horse show as we launched the canoe on a weekday in late June. At the first bend a great blue heron pushed skyward from his perch on a dead tree overhanging the river, and a mother mallard and her brood drifted with the current and then disappeared into streamside brush. The voice from the horse show loudspeaker faded into the sound of the river and the rustle of the wind in the trees. We were alone on the most famous trout stream in the Adirondacks ... and fish were rising everywhere.

Joe Hackett is one of a new breed of Adirondack guides. Like many of the guides before him, he grew up in the Adirondacks where he learned to fish and hunt and find his way through the mountains. But unlike his predecessors, Joe earned a college degree in recreation and has devoted considerable time and money to learn the finer points of canoeing, fly fishing, cross country skiing, living in the wilderness and working—and playing—with people.

I met Joe when he started his guiding career more than 10 years ago, and we've been friends ever since. He lives with his wife, Maria and their daughters, Willow and Meadow in Raybrook, NY, about halfway between Lake Placid and Saranac Lake.

When I was planning this book on canoe-fishing, I asked Joe if he could spend a few days showing me how and where its done in his area of the Adirondacks. Although his specialty is packing into remote ponds in search of brook trout, he agreed to show me some easywater where almost anyone can canoe and catch fish. We canoe-fished the Ausable, Saranac and Boquet Rivers, each offering a different taste of the Adirondacks.

The Ausable near Lake Placid is a mountain stream that runs over granite and gravel as it winds its way from pool to riffle, eastward towards the Champlain Valley. Evergreens and hardwoods, and an assortment of shrubs and spring flowers push tightly to the river's banks in most areas.

Whiteface Mountain overlooks this stretch of river, but we couldn't see it the first morning because of the clouds that hung low in the mountains. But, the light rain that dimpled the water seemed to turn on the trout in every pool. Joe drifted nymphs to these rising fish and I enticed them with spinners and small plugs. We both caught fish, nothing big.

Joe explained that because this stream is so popular, the state stocks it quite heavily with three species of trout. Most of the fish we caught were recently stocked fish, but a few had some real color. In the crystal clear water we could see bigger fish that just weren't interested. Joe noted that when there is an especially good hatch these big trout can be had, especially the ones in waters away from the road.

Even on this rainy weekday, there was a fisherman or two in almost every roadside pool. A few ventured upstream or down but none of them were fishing the holes where we caught fish.

I wore hip boots, but Joe knew that the river offered many areas where it was easy to fish from shore or from water that was only a couple of inches deep, so he wore ankle high pacs.

We took our time, fishing from the canoe and wading a few stretches that roadside fishermen couldn't reach, and we still finished by noon. A perfect stretch of water for a morning or evening run.

We returned the next day—when the sun decided to shine—to take some photographs. Whiteface Mountain looked down on us through a midday haze. The river was beautiful. Not a single fish dimpled the surface.

While we were playing the game of starting the timer on the camera, jumping into the canoe and casting to a midstream rock, a foot-long rainbow trout hit my Phoebe and jumped three times before the camera decided to take the picture.

The best way to locate the launch and take out sites is with a "New York State Atlas & Gazetteer" or topo maps of the areas. If you prefer a guided trip, call Joe Hackett at 518-891-4334, or write to him at Tahawus Guide Service, Box 424, Lake Placid, NY 12946. For information on accommodations and attractions in the area write to: Lake Placid Chamber of Commerce, Olympic Arena, Lake Placid, NY 12946.

SARANAC RIVER

Despite the on and off rain, we launched the canoe on the Saranac River just north of the village of Saranac Lake off Route 3. I was canoe-fishing with long time friend and Adirondack guide, Joe Hackett. He noted that this trip required almost no canoeing skills, offered some good fishing and the opportunity to see a variety of wildlife. My kind of place.

This stretch of river starts with a rush near the launch site, but quickly slows to a meander as it winds through a gently sloping Adirondack valley. Here swamp grasses, cattails and wetland flowers push to the water's edge.

Northern pike, smallmouth and largemouth bass, rockbass and other sunfish inhabit these waters. Joe noted that this is where he canoe-fishes when his clients want their children to catch lots of fish.

The rain stopped and a patchwork of clouds turned the sun on and off as a weather front slowly moved through the area. Fish don't like cold fronts even in June. We tried spinners, spoons, plugs, and live minnows. One small northern pike followed a lure to the canoe. We didn't raise another fish on the first half of the trip.

"Further downstream there are some deep holes and rocks. Maybe we'll find fish there", Joe explained as we paddled and fished only the most likely waters. Mallards in flights of ones and twos winged overhead, a great blue heron waded a shallow bay, red-wing blackbirds complained, and an immature bald eagle lifted off a lonesome tree and effortlessly flew down river—a rare sight in the Adirondacks.

The Saranac was a much-used river. Over the years its waters floated logs and powered a variety of mills. The remnants of old dams, buildings and bridges attest to the importance that water played in the settlement of the region. Today, at least in this area, the power of the river is less important.

We finally found fish near the remnants of an old dam. Some small bass took our lures in the upstream pool. The big fish were on the bottom of a deeper pool on the downstream side. We hooked, caught and lost several big smallmouths by bouncing yellow plastic jigs off the bottom.

Joe was visibly relieved. He had bragged up this stretch of river so much and we just couldn't find fish that were hungry or angry enough to attack our lures until our trip was almost over.

The Saranac changed near the old dam. There was more current, more rocks, and spruce, cedar and pine bordered the river. We saw plenty of deer and raccoon tracks in the mud, and beaver sign was everywhere. I was sorry we were approaching our take-out vehicle.

We took a half day to cover about three miles, but could have made it a day trip by taking out further downstream. The river runs close to Route 3, so it's relatively easy to take out in a number of places. We ended our trip at an old bridge on a dirt road about a quarter mile from the highway.

There are many places to buy tackle in this area, but nothing compares to the Blue Line Sportshop right in the village of Saranac Lake. Sam Grimone took me on a tour of two floors of outdoor gear and tackle. I bought some fishing lures, topo maps and some camping gear. I'll be back.

For information on accommodations in this area write: Saranac Lake Chamber of Commerce, 30 Main St., Saranac Lake, NY 12983. For a guided trip, write: Joe Hackett, Box 424, Lake Placid, NY 12946.

BOQUET RIVER

It didn't seem like an Adirondack Mountain river. From where we stood it looked like any flat valley stream in central or western New York. There were no rocks, no rapids, no wild forests, just a shallow, meandering stream through a beautiful country valley.

Joe Hackett explained that if the water was higher, we could launch right there in Pleasant Valley and fish from New Russia right through Elizabethtown to Wadhams Rd. He noted that some areas of this section are very good for trout, but it would be tough to get through with a canoe in low water, so we would launch below E-Town.

Joe grew up on the Boquet River in this area, so he knows it well, perhaps better than any other Adirondack guide. Most guides and fishermen on the Boquet prefer the more popular downstream waters during the landlocked-salmon fall spawning runs.

The lack of attention to upstream waters, except by local anglers, makes the Boquet River ideal for canoe-fishermen. DEC stocks thousands of brown and rainbow trout, and some brook trout near bridges and in areas where roads and river come together. Many of these fish are caught near the stocking points, but a fair number move into less accessible areas where they grow fat on abundant insects and minnows. Some natural reproduction adds to this population of "wild" trout.

Like most New York streams the Boquet flows through areas that few bank or wading fishermen ever see, so it holds pockets of fish that almost never see lures or bait. We were looking for those fish when we launched the canoe near the intersection of Coonrod and Pierce Roads, northwest of Wadhams, about 8 AM in late June. This would be a short run to Clark Road just north of Route 22 in Wadhams.

While Joe flycast nymphs, I tried to connect with spinners and small plugs. Except for a few small trout, our morning run was a bust.

Bust turned to boon that afternoon.

I really believe you have to pay your dues for things to work out right. It's happened to me so many times. You know what I mean—nothing goes right, be it fishing, hunting, canoeing or camping, but for some reason you stick it out, get through the bad without giving

Except for an occasional rock outcrop the Boquet River looked like a flat-valley stream in the areas Joe Hackett and I canoe-fished for trout and bass.

Schroon River offers some interesting canoeing water and the opportunity to take some nice bass and trout. This smallmouth bass held by Paul Gibaldi couldn't resist a crayfish plug that swam over a submerged log.

up, and then everything seems to turn around. That was the case on the Boquet that early summer morning—we paid our dues.

After lunch in Willsboro, we parked one vehicle at the bridge near the hamlet of Boquet, just off Route 22 on Jersey Road, and drove upstream (south on 22) to launch the canoe at Wallonsburg. The river was different here, more current, more rocks, more trees ... and more hungry fish.

Deer tracks were everywhere in the soft sand and mud. An owl (in flight they look like a headless hawk to me) lifted from a down-stream tree and pumped out of sight. Further downstream an osprey screeched in protest as it gave up it's perch.

After our disappointing morning run, Joe switched from nymphs to live minnows. He cast a lip-hooked minnow just above holding water, let it drift downstream, twitching the rod tip during the drift and during the retrieve. Sometimes he used a sinker, some-times none, depending on the depth and speed of the water.

I stuck with a crayfish plug. I cranked just fast enough to allow the plug to hit bottom from time to time. In some areas I could see fish chasing the plug and feel them grabbing it. Damn that felt good! One problem, the hooks on that little plug were so small I lost almost as many fish as I caught.

We caught brown trout, rainbow trout, smallmouth bass and river shad. No monsters, but enough 10 inchers to make our light tackle dance and sing.

We were drifting around a long bend in the river, casting to a pool on the outside turn, when we heard a "rumble" in the distance.

"Was that thunder?"

The answer came almost as fast as the question, as a herd of a dozen horses galloped along the river, just outside the trees that lined the bank.

"Nice touch, Joe. How did you arrange that?", I quipped.

We didn't see another canoe and only a handful of fishermen on the entire trip, morning and afternoon. Of course this was a week-day and well into the trout season, a time when local fishermen had to work or had their fill of catching fish.

Many areas of the Boquet cannot be fished from a canoe. There are long stretches of rapids and boulders and waterfalls that are major obstacles to canoe-fishing. The stretches noted here are easywater and pose little danger except during spring runoff or other high water periods.

The Boquet is famous for its landlocked Atlantic salmon spawning runs and hundreds of anglers flock to the lower reaches of the river each fall. DEC maintains a fish ladder to allow the salmon access to the waters above the waterfalls at Willsboro. There is a special viewing window that is a must-see for anyone interested in fish or fishing.

For information on accommodations and attractions in the area write: Lake Placid/Essex County Vistor's Bureau, Olympic Center, Lake Placid, NY 12946. For a guided trip write: Joe Hackett, Box 424, Lake Placid, NY 12946.

GRASSE RIVER

"What kind of canoe-fishing is this?", I wondered; knee-deep in water with a canoe tied to my belt and a leaping smallmouth at the end of an ultralight spinning rig.

Mike Seymour and I were fishing the Grasse River where it flows into the St. Lawrence Valley over limestone bedrock in a series of shallow rapids and small waterfalls. The smallmouths were hanging tight to the fast water where there was plenty of oxygen, so the only way we could get to them was to wade. The canoe came along for the ride tied to my belt or left to drift downstream ahead of us. When we found an especially productive area, we pulled the canoe up on a rock ledge. The only time we actually got in the canoe was to paddle to the next section of rapids.

Mike Seymour is a teacher, outdoor writer and fishing guide who lives in Heuvelton, NY with his wife, Mary Sue and two sons. He has written about his fishing and hunting adventures in the regional section of the NEW YORK SPORTSMAN for several years, so I asked him to take me canoe-fishing in his area.

Mike had warned me that this would be a different kind of canoe-fishing when we made plans to fish the Grasse in mid July.

"The water will be warm so you won't need waders. Wear sneakers and plan to be in the water most of the time."

Up until then my canoe-fishing experiences had included some wading, but most of the time I had fished from the canoe. That was impossible on this stretch of the Grasse River.

We put the canoe in at the Niagara Mohawk cartop launch a mile upstream from Chamberlain Corners off County Route 55 an hour after sunrise and paddled downstream to the first rapids.

We had emptied our pockets of wallets and such and stored them in ziplock bags in day packs. We both wore long pants, light long sleeved shirts, sneakers and ball caps. I carried my fishing tackle in a vest, Mike kept his in his pockets. While he preferred a 6-foot plus medium-action spinning outfit, I stuck with a 5 1/2-foot ultralight rig.

Most of the time we waded in knee-deep water, but on occasion we got wet to the waist. In the heat of the day it felt great. The Grasse was quite wide in most areas of shallow, fast water, so we separated, Mike fishing the left side of the river and I the right. We crisscrossed our sides of the stream, occasionally casting to the same water in midstream. We found fish in pools below waterfalls, in pockets near boulders and in slick water just out of the main current. We took lots of fish, none of them very big, but on ultralight tackle a 10 inch smallmouth that lives in fast water can jump and run like a grown-up fish. We caught dozens of these small bass and a couple of 12-13 inchers. I can't remember having more fun on a hot summer day.

Depending on the depth of the water which ranged from a few inches to three or four feet, we caught smallmouths, rockbass and fallfish on spinners, spoons, plugs and plastic jigs. Spinners like the Mepps, Blue Fox, Panther Martin and C.P. Swing, and the Phoebe spoon did the trick in most areas, but in a few deep holes plastic jigs and crayfish plugs produced fish.

Mike noted that the slower, deeper waters between rapids also hold respectable-size muskies and some northern pike, but we didn't fish for them or catch any by accident.

In some areas the vegetation growing on the rock-hard bottom was short and thick, and felt like a plush carpet under foot. I doubt if that was the reason they called this stream the Grasse, but I had never seen so much thick underwater stream "grass" in New York State.

Mike Seymour minds the canoe while we fish a series of rapids on the Grasse River for smallmouth bass.

We both caught 3-pound walleyes at Remington Rapids on the Oswegatchie River.

It took all morning to cover the three miles to our take-out at Chase Mills because we waded most of the way. After we loaded the canoe on our downstream vehicle and returned to get the vehicle at the launch site, we drove upstream to the village of Madrid where we had lunch at a diner. From there we drove further upstream to Morely and started to fish a similar stretch of water to Buck's Bridge. We never finished that leg of our trip. We got into so many smallmouths we ran out of time only a mile from the launch site, so we towed the canoe back to the car, casting on occasion to the still hungry smallmouths.

OSWEGATCHIE RIVER

I could hardly sleep the night before canoe-fishing the Oswegatchie River. I had fished from Heuvelton to Eel Weir State Park many times, so I knew how productive this lower area of the Oswegatchie could be. I was not familiar with the stretches above Heuvelton, so I asked Mike Seymour to guide me on a section of the river where the canoeing was easy and the fish were hungry.

Mike picked the stretch from Rensselaer Falls to Heuvelton because I had never fished it before and because he had always fished it from an outboard powered boat that couldn't get to the water near the Remington Rapids. So, this was an adventure for both of us.

We launched off Route 59 just downstream from Rensselaer Falls. Early morning sunlight filtered through shoreline trees, creating varying patterns of shade and light as the barely perceptible current carried us along. We cast to logs, downed willows and to small points and bays. Mepps spinners took a small northern pike and a few smallmouth bass. For the first three hours fishing was terrible.

But this was canoe-fishing so it didn't matter. Summer-green willows, maples and box elders, outlined by a deep blue sky provided shade from the rising sun, and shrubs, grasses and flowers passed by as we drifted and paddled downstream. Great blue herons, ducks, crows and kingfishers scolded and entertained us along the way. We had shifted gears from serious fishing to just enjoying the feel of the canoe and the river, the sights and sounds of nature, and the taking of a fish now and then. We were in for a surprise. Two surprises actually.

As we approached Remington Rapids, midstream boulders broke the surface of the water and announced a significant change in the character of the river. We dropped to our knees to run a short rapids. This first barrier to powerboats drops into a long stretch of deeper water that ends with another, longer rapids and more boulders, that block the path of powerboats from downstream. We stopped below the upstream rapids to eat lunch, for Mike to take a swim ... and to fish.

The slick water below and to the sides of the rapids were loaded with small bass and rockbass. Mike caught most of his fish on a blue tube jig, so before we launched the canoe and paddled across the river to fish deeper water, I switched from a crankbait to a chartreuse curlytail jig.

Surprise! Mike's rod bent to the river and the drag on his spinning reel gave up line in short gasps as a heavy fish tried to stay on the bottom. This was serious business. I paddled the canoe from the bow as Mike worked the fish to the surface. It was a golden, 3-pound walleye.

After we ran the downstream rapids and started bouncing jigs among the boulders, we were discussing how surprised we were to catch such a nice walleye in the middle of the summer in this area when ... **Surprise!** My rod tip took a nose dive and another 3-pound walleye reluctantly came to the side of the canoe.

The sun was getting high and hot, and we had just tangled with two walleyes that any river fisherman would be proud to catch, so I suggested that we take a few pictures and call it quits on a high note. Mike agreed, so we paddled the last half mile to the roadside parking area just upstream from the village of Heuvelton.

Mike and I merely sampled the canoe-fishing opportunities on the Grasse and Oswegatchie rivers. There are miles and miles of productive water that can be fished from or reached with a canoe.

The Department of Environmental Conservation publishes Fishing and Canoeing booklets on the Grasse, Oswegatchie and other rivers in this area. For a copy write to: Regional Fisheries Manager, NYSDEC, Dept CFB, 317 Washington St., Watertown, NY 13601-3787. For information on accommodations and attractions write to: St. Lawrence County Chamber of Commerce, Dept. MPK,Drawer A, Canton, NY 13617. Mike Seymour's address is Box 376, 7 Rensselaer St. Heuvelton, NY 13654.

We paid our dues on the Black River near Lyons Falls ... and found walleyes and smallmouth bass. I didn't have to ask Denny Gillen to smile when he caught this 15 1/2 inch bass on a floating Rapala.

Pete Hornbeck's 15-pound, 10-foot canoes were ideal for fishing the Kunjamuk River ... and getting over beaver dams.

SCHROON RIVER

The mountain stream turned sharply to the right, pushed tight to a granite outcrop and descended into a deep pool. With a little help the canoe made it through without a hitch, punched a hole in the eddy line and drifted into calm water. We were so wrapped up in the beauty of the river and the fun of canoeing we forgot a cardinal rule of canoe-fishing ... and spooked every bass and trout in the river.

There are hundreds of miles of New York streams that rush and meander through some of the most populated and developed areas of the state, yet they can provide exceptional canoe-fishing opportunities. Contrasting these civilized streams are the mountain waters of the Adirondacks where people and roads are few and far between. I have enjoyed canoe-fishing both kinds of streams, but had never canoe-fished a stream that was in the Adirondack Mountains ... AND ... a stones throw from one of the most heavily traveled highways in the north—until I canoe-fished the Schroon River.

Thousands of New Yorkers drive the Northway (Route I-87) between Albany and Canada each year. While most of them are very familiar with Schroon Lake, only a few realize that the ribbon of water that parallels the highway, north and south of the lake, is the Schroon River. Almost no one knows that much of this stream is ideal canoe-fishing water.

Paul Gibaldi is an Adirondack fishing guide who lives near the Schroon River south of Schroon Lake, and although his specialty is fishing Adirondack ponds and lakes, he agreed to guide me on a canoe-fishing adventure on the Schroon River.

Actually it was two canoe-fishing adventures. The first started at the New York State Boat Launch near the village of Pottersville, not far from the Schroon Lake outlet. This section of stream is perfect water for novice canoe-fishermen because it meanders for five miles to the Starbuckville Dam. Paul and I didn't have the time to cover the entire five miles, so we put in at the boat launch, canoe-fished downstream for two hours and then canoe-fished back. The current was so slight it was easy paddling upstream, making this stretch ideal for someone with only one vehicle or limited fishing time. It's also a good place to canoe-fish during those productive couple of hours in the morning and evening. Unfortunately, we weren't able to fish those hours.

Weed-lined banks, small bays and sunken logs provide ideal cover for bass, pickerel and northern pike. The pickerel and pike were on holiday while we were there, but some bass smacked our plugs, spinners and spinner baits even with the sun high and bright.

I get turned on by sunken logs, having caught some nice fish over the years from such shaded havens. I wasn't disappointed here either. The water was crystal clear where I plopped a small crank-bait just beyond a huge log that was partially suspended in four feet of water. Just before my make-believe crayfish climbed over that log, a big bass ate it ... and provided a sample of the fishing this area can offer canoeing fishermen.

Another plus for fishing so close to Schroon Lake is the possibility of catching rainbow, brown and lake trout, or landlocked salmon. This is especially so during the spring when the river is high and cold.

Spruce, birch, cedar, alders and a variety of flowers and other plantlife line the banks and form weedbeds in this area, providing excellent habitat for great blue heron, mallards and black ducks. They are fun to watch anytime of year, but are most active during late spring and early summer.

Our second adventure started downstream at Riverbank near Northway Exit 24. Canoe access is off River Road, just north of the County Highway 11 Bridge, on the east side of the river. Although this stretch is canoeable for 10 miles to County Home Bridge, we opted for a shorter trip. We found a couple of spots to take out along River Road and picked one about five miles downstream. Paul parked his truck well off the road and we returned to the launch site in my Jeep.

This was my kind of canoe-fishing—free-flowing water that provides enough current to move the canoe along and just enough obstacles to test my limited canoeing skills. Of course these same obstacles also provide fish habitat.

At first we connected with the fish that were feeding in the log-infested pools and deep runs, but as water depth decreased and clarity increased our success plummeted. We saw an occasional fish, but absolutely nothing would hit our lures.

Paul had recently purchased a Radison canoe. He had used it exclusively to fish Adirondack ponds and lakes, so it didn't have a scratch on it. I couldn't resist kidding him about it, especially when he groaned when we bottomed out going through a short riffle.

"No one will believe this is an Adirondack guide's canoe if it doesn't have a few scratches and dents in it. You won't have to worry about that after today. It'll get christened for sure."

Paul groaned again, and again as the canoe scraped bottom and occasionally bounced off a rock as we negotiated a series of riffles and pools. When we stopped on a gravel bar for lunch he didn't even wince when the canoe "ground" to a halt. The canoe and Paul were ready for some real fun.

This stretch of the Schroon River is especially beautiful. Maple, oak and some huge white pine tower over the water. During the spring wildflowers grow near the water's edge. Outcrops of Adirondack granite speak of eons of glaciation and water-wear, and ensure the permanence of the course of the river in this area.

Except when passing under a Northway bridge or coming close enough to the highway to hear the traffic, we seemed to be deep in the wilderness.

Once the canoe was christened and Paul and I learned to work together, we really got into running riffles and short rapids. When we didn't have a paddle in our hands, we cast a variety of lures for the bass and trout we knew were there, but didn't realize until later why we couldn't catch fish.

A fast-moving shadow spooks fish, and that's just what our canoe presented to every fish in the river as we bombed through feeding areas. If the river was high and dirty, it would have forgiven such stupidity, but it was low and clear. Even a novice stream fisherman knows enough to stay low and downstream when casting to such fish havens as the head and tail waters of pools. Canoe-fishermen who really want to catch fish in such water, have to beach the canoe upstream, walk downstream and fish back to the canoe.

I knew that. Paul knew that. We just weren't paying attention. That's what's so great about canoe-fishing. You don't have to do everything right, you don't have to catch a bunch of fish to have fun. The feel of the canoe, the sights and sounds of the river, the smell of clean air and wildflowers, the antics of streamside birds and other wildlife, all add up to make canoe-fishing fun even when the fish are lockjawed.

If you don't buy all that, and really want to catch fish in this area of the Schroon River, canoe-fish it during the months of May, June, sometimes July, and again in late September or October when the water is high and not so clear. Live bait is deadly on all game fish. Worms and minnows are best for trout, while crayfish and minnows are best for bass. In the deeper pools diving plugs, spinner baits, heavy spoons and jigs will do the job. Spinners, floating plugs and spoons will take fish in shallow water. Keep in mind that bass season doesn't open until the third Saturday in June.

Almost no canoeing skills are required on the stretch between Pottersville and Starbuckville Dam. The run starting at Riverbank requires only limited canoeing skills, except during the spring runoff when most Adirondack streams can be very dangerous to canoeing fishermen.

Incidentally, there is a stretch of the Schroon River between the areas we canoe-fished that harbors some big brown and rainbow trout. Trouble is, the area is so heavily posted, it's almost impossible to get on and off the river with a canoe. However, Paul Gibaldi has made special arrangements for access to this area, so he can canoe-fish it with his clients.

For more information about this area of New York State write to: Warren County Department of Tourism 795 Municipal Center, Lake George, NY 12845-9795 or call 518-761-6366. For a guided trip write to: Gibaldi Guide Service, H.C.R. # 2, 121D Schroon River Rd., Warrensburg, NY 12885.

BLACK RIVER

Despite the fact that we hadn't caught a single fish in over two hours, Denny continued to cast his perch Rapala. During that same period I tried spinners, spoons, plastic jigs and a crayfish crankbait with equal success. Fortunately for us the feel of the canoe and the sights and sounds of the river more than made up for the lousy fishing. We didn't complain, however, when the bass and walleyes started eating lures later that afternoon.

Choosing a five-mile stretch of the Black River for a day of canoe-fishing wasn't easy. Most of the upstream trout water is not canoeable and the cool-water downstream stretches move too slow for my kind of—let the current do the work—canoe-fishing. Sure there are a number of upstream runs that can be canoe-fished, but they are short in length and if you don't know exactly where to put in and take out, they can be dangerous. Likewise there are miles of downstream runs that offer some fine canoe-fishing if you like to paddle and don't mind the competition of powerboat anglers. So a compromise was required to find a section of the Black River for a day of reasonably good fishing and easy-water canoeing without the hassle of powerboats. With the help of some stream and road maps, a scouting trip and a call to the DEC Watertown Office, I found what I was looking for and then some.

For Denny Gillen and I this was sort of a celebration. In the past year he had survived major surgery and retired from the Rome, NY Fire Department. During that same period I too had been under the surgeon's scalpel and retired from the Federal Aviation Administration. We had much to be thankful for—we were alive and had the time to canoe-fish when we wanted to if our wives (sisters they be) didn't have anything else for us to do.

We had planned a midweek outing to avoid the "crowds", but mother nature canceled that, so we drove north to canoe-fish the Black River on one of the most popular outdoor days of the year— Sunday on Labor Day weekend. I could just picture a fleet of canoes at the Canoe Launch below Lyons Falls.

It was 37 degrees and a cold mist hung over New York's northern rivers, so we lingered over breakfast coffee and discussed what I had learned from Fisheries Biologist, Doug Carlson. Doug had explained that the river below Lyons Falls all the way to Carthage is home to walleyes, bass, rockbass, plus some northern pike, pickerel and yellow perch. The five-mile stretch I was interested in was, for the most part, slow moving water over a sandy bottom. Doug noted that the waters near natural rock outcrops and bridge abutments were the best places to find concentrations of fish.

After leaving Denny's truck at the parking area just downstream from the bridge at Burdick's Crossing, we launched the canoe below Lyons Falls. Surprise! Surprise! There were no cars in the Canoe Launch parking lot and only one truck down near the river. Two anglers were fishing below the falls. We paddled over to the falls on the side where the paper mill water outlets boiled into the river. Great looking water! We fished the outlets, below the falls opposite the two shore anglers, and in the large downstream pool. No fish.

As we drifted from the fall's pool and a gentle current grabbed the canoe, we settled in for a day on the Black River. It was 10 a.m., temperature about 60 degrees, bright sun, fluffy white clouds and a deep blue sky. A great blue heron flew overhead and announced our presence with a squawk.

Our plan was to paddle to the areas that Doug Carlson had mentioned, cast lures most of the time, and drift nightcrawlers through the best looking holes for walleyes. For the first couple of hours Denny did most of the casting with his perch Rapala. I kept the canoe in the current and away from midstream obstructions. It was very easy canoeing. Just enough current to do the work, but slow enough so I could cast from time to time.

More surprises. We didn't see a single home or camp, not even a farm house for the first two hours of the trip. The shoreline was a forest of oak, maple, box elder, hemlock, plus a few willow and white pine. Rock outcrops were few and far between, but we fished them hard with lures and occasionally with worms. Not a nibble.

About a mile below Lyons Falls we could hear the rush of a rapids or waterfalls but couldn't see any indications of rock outcrops or a narrowing river. To be on the safe side we hugged the shoreline until we could see a downstream V that passed through the far left side of a barrier that crossed the river. It was a wooden dam that lifted the river a couple of feet. If the water was a few inches higher we could have passed over it anywhere, a few inches lower and we would have had to carry around it. The water below the dam looked too good to pass up. We could almost feel the smallmouths that had to be there sucking up all that oxygen. Not one hit.

Downstream from the wooden dam we had to work our way through rows of pilings that crossed the river in some places and ran parallel to the shore in others. I learned later that these pilings are the remnants of a canal navigation channel that ran between Lyons Falls and Carthage on the Black River through 1920. Some of these piles were just under the water, so I imagine they have jolted more than one canoeist and eaten the props off a few outboard motors. The current in this area is very slow, so they are easily avoided with a watchful eye and minimal canoeing skills.

We passed a small bass boat that had motored up from a downstream launch. Two anglers were fishing worms and had caught a small walleye and a perch. The day before their live bait had taken a 4 1/2 pound walleye. There was hope for this river after all.

Our next stop was three stone bridge abutments (Whittlesly Bridge), an especially productive area according to Doug Carlson. Just upstream from this long abandoned crossing is the only house on the entire section of river. A pair of yellow Labrador retrievers announced our arrival, and the owners inquired about our success thus far. It turns out they had been too busy tearing down an old house and building a new one to enjoy the fishing in their own backyard.

We decided to stop near the abutments for lunch and to dunk a few worms for walleyes. As we passed by the east shore abutment Denny cast his Rapala and hooked the first fish of the day—a golden walleye about 14 inches long. Things were looking up.

During lunch Denny's worm took a fallfish. After lunch we fished all three abutments and the waters upstream and down without success. Hotspot? Couldn't prove it by us.

When a merganser "pumped" her way up the other side of the river, Denny joked about how hungry she must be on this fishless water.

A mile or so downstream from the old abutments we drifted into a long deep run next to a rocky outcrop. At the upstream end of the run were some weeds growing next to the rocks. As we cast to the edge of the weeds on our left, a minnow surfaced in deeper water on our right. I dropped a curly tail jig into the deeper water and had it almost back to the canoe when a fish nearly yanked the rod out of my hand. I lost that fish, but a couple minutes later hooked and landed a 15-inch walleye.

Denny continued to cast his favorite lure tight to the rock outcrop. Just downstream from the weeds, a good fish ate his lure and dove to deeper water. The fish boiled the water next to the canoe and dove for the bottom three times before being lifted from the river. We spent the next five minutes positioning the canoe so I could take pictures of Denny and his 2-pound, 15 1/2 inch Black River smallmouth. I didn't have to tell Denny to smile.

Such a spot deserved another run. Denny took two more bass. A good fish grabbed my plastic jig, dove to the bottom and circled the back of the canoe where I was sitting. With the rod over my head, I tried to reach back to work the fish around the stern of the canoe. It didn't work.

While we fought, lost, landed and took pictures of fish beside that very productive rocky outcrop, a canoe and a small boat passed by. We checked the time. It was three o'clock and we had more than a mile to paddle to Burdick's Crossing. We had planned to head home by four. This lower section of the river was barely moving and there was a fair wind blowing upstream, so we dug in with our paddles and covered water.

We passed the canoe and the small boat powered by an electric motor. A mallard lifted off the river and a kingfisher complained as it flew overhead. Cornstalks lay in the river, dragged there by beavers or raccoons no doubt. The paddles felt good in our hands as the canoe sliced the surface of the river.

It was great to be alive.

For more information on this area of New York State write: Lewis County Chamber of Commerce, 7550 State St. Lowville, NY 13367.

KUNJAMUK RIVER

It was next to the last day of trout season when Pete Hornbeck and I met for breakfast at The Cafe in Speculator. We had planned to spend the day canoe-fishing nearby Kunjamuk River for brook trout, bass and pickerel. It was pouring rain at 9 a.m., so there was no hurry to launch the canoes.

Pete is the founder, owner and main man (usually the only man) at Hornbeck Boats in Olmstedville, NY where he makes canoes and guideboats. His most popular craft is a 10-foot kevlar canoe that weighs a mere 15 pounds. A friend told me that Pete was a fishing fanatic who canoe-fished throughout the Adirondacks using his one-man canoes. While vacationing in nearby Schroon Lake I visited Pete's shop and paddled one of those "mini" canoes around his pond. I was impressed by their ease of handling and stability, but not convinced they would work for me in a free-flowing stream. Pete accepted the challenge to show me, hence our meeting to fish the Kunjamuk.

While it poured outside, we talked canoeing and fishing, and about Pete's canoes. It rained and rained, and we talked and talked until downpour turned to drizzle around noon. Nice people at The Cafe.

I parked my vehicle next to the Sacandaga River across from the outlet of the Kunjamuk off Route 30, east of Speculator. Pete ,with two canoes in his pickup, drove us back to town, turned right at the Route 8/Route 30 intersection, continued north on this road until the pavement ended, took the first fork to the right and followed that road until we reached the river at a gravel pit. Although this is International Paper Company land, access is permitted for fishing and canoeing.

It was still raining, so we donned rain gear and sneakers and unloaded the canoes. Except for a couple of tours around the pond I had never been in a one man-canoe before, so while Pete parked his truck, I looked it over. Quite spartan really. Ten-feet long, 27 inches wide in the middle and pointed at both ends. Except for the wood around the gunnel, the padded thwart that served as a backrest and the foam seat on the bottom, the canoe was all kevlar. That, of course, is why it weighs only 15 pounds.

Anxious to try the canoe on the river and to fish, I put my pack-basket in the back of the canoe and tied it to the thwart, and then rigged one rod with a crayfish plug and the other with a spinner.

The only time the canoe felt unstable was while getting into it, so as instructed, I put it parallel to shore in shallow water, sat down and then pushed off. A few sweeps of the double paddle and I was around the bend making my first cast.

My first few casts produced weeds, grass actually, so I changed the lure on the "plug" rod to a floating Rapala. A cast next to a bank of solid alders produced a hit and a fish that rolled on the surface and was gone. The flash of color looked like a brook trout to me, but that may be wishful thinking because for the next half-hour every-thing we threw in that stretch of river was gobbled up by a pickerel. It was great fun for awhile, but we wanted to catch some trout and bass, so the deeper, less weedy downstream runs beckoned.

Pete had fished this river before and had taken some nice small-mouths. One of his friends had caught a—get this—a 20-inch plus bass that weighed over five pounds. A friend of mine told me he had caught a trout, bass and a pickerel out of the same hole on the Kun-jamuk. That's good fishing.

The rain stopped for awhile and the sun popped through the clouds, lighting up the hardwood forest and streamside vegetation that was ablaze with color. Yellow birch and red maple against the backdrop of dark green hemlock was spectacular. The bright red berries of mountain ash and the yellows and reds of trees and brush reflected in pools and backsets as we cast spinners and plugs in search of elusive bass and trout. At the time we didn't realize that the change in weather was caused by a slowly moving cold front.

The Kunjamuk is a narrow, winding mountain stream that is beaver heaven. Beaver sign is everywhere, including countless slides that tunnel through alders, fresh cuttings and lots of beaver dams. We worked the waters above and below old and new dams. A few bumps, a couple of hits got our hopes up, but those cooperative fish turned out to be fallfish, or Mohawk chubs as they are called in this area. No bass, no trout.

Pete and I developed a leapfrog approach to fishing this narrow river. I paddled past two or three good-looking holes and runs, so he could fish them. When he caught up to me, he passed through, by-passing a few good looking areas, and so on downstream. Our technique didn't wake up any bass or trout, but it did get us into more fallfish and pickerel. We caught most of the pickerel near weeds or at the mouths of weedy bays and most of the fallfish in the runs and pools below fast water. Pete took the biggest fish, a 20-inch pickerel.

The only problem I had with the canoe was holding it in the current so I could cast. Sometimes I could position the canoe in an eddy or beach it. On occasion I tucked the branch of an alder under my arm to hold the canoe. Pete solved this problem with a short length of rope and a carpenter's spring clamp that he clipped to the alders. He said he couldn't find another clamp for the canoe I was using. Sure.

We didn't see much wildlife, just a few ducks. One black duck didn't even blink as we drifted by. It was far more interested in pulling vegetation off the bottom. Of course it was difficult to see past the almost impenetrable alders that lined the river in most areas.

Around five o'clock we had reached the really deep holes and runs where we should have concentrated our efforts using deep-diving crankbaits, spinner baits, plastic jigs or bait, but it started raining hard again and we were cold and tired. We had been on the river for five hours, and thinking and talking canoe-fishing for over eight hours. Dry feet, a hot bowl of soup and a cup of coffee sounded mighty good all of a sudden. With double paddles in high gear it didn't take long to cover that last mile of river and cross Kunjamuk Bay to the takeout.

Over dinner at The Inn in Speculator we talked about what we should have done. We should have paddled up the river, fishing the deeper runs and holes before the cold front moved through. Then we would have caught lots of bass and maybe even some trout. We agreed, however, that despite the rain, catching pickerel and fallfish was great fun, the beauty of the fall foliage was spectacular and canoeing the Kunjamuk in tiny boats was a unique outdoor adventure.

For information on Pete's canoes write: Pete Hornbeck, Box 23, Troutbrook Rd., Olmstedville, NY 12857. For more information on the Kunjamuk River write: Office of Tourism, Speculator, NY 12164.

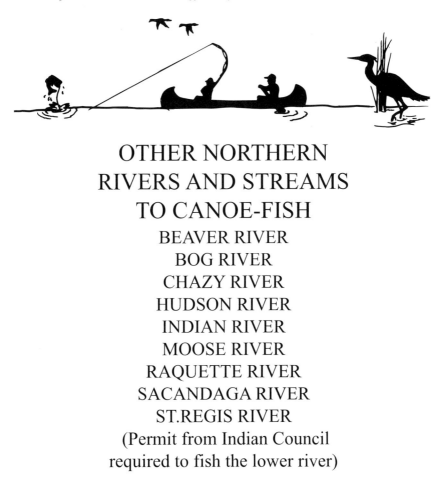

OTHER NORTHERN RIVERS AND STREAMS TO CANOE-FISH

BEAVER RIVER
BOG RIVER
CHAZY RIVER
HUDSON RIVER
INDIAN RIVER
MOOSE RIVER
RAQUETTE RIVER
SACANDAGA RIVER
ST.REGIS RIVER
(Permit from Indian Council
required to fish the lower river)

CHAPTER 10

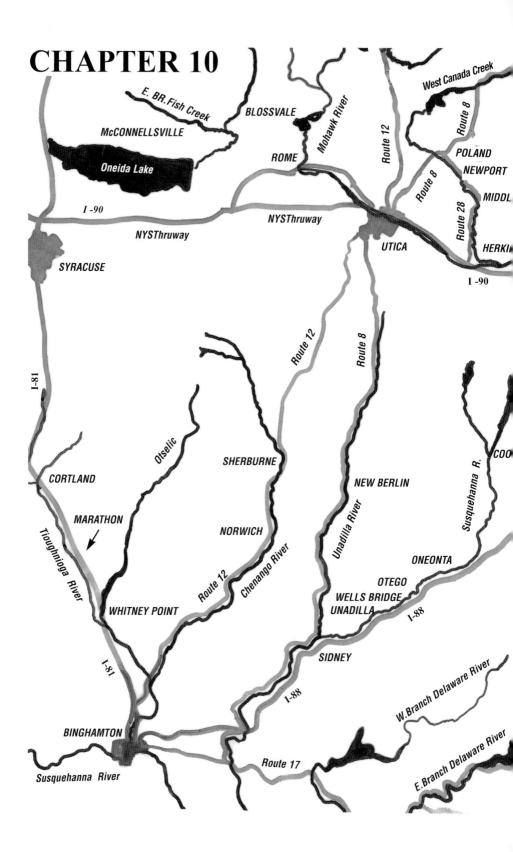

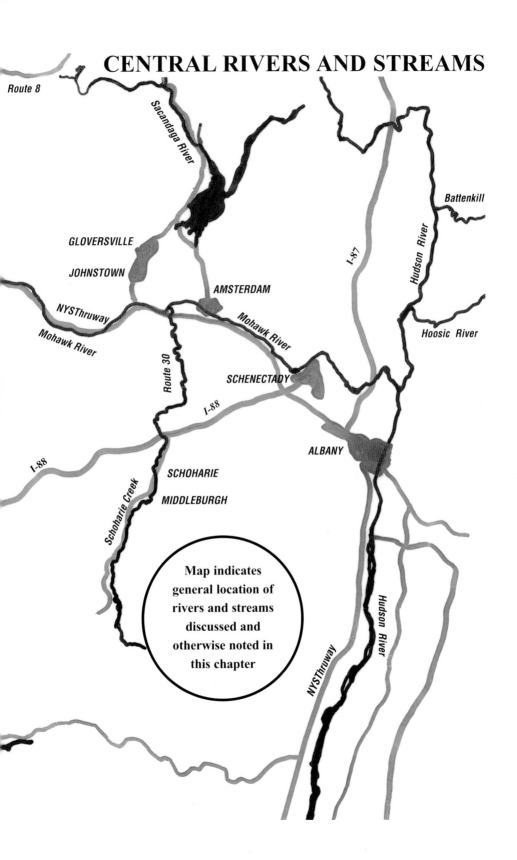

CENTRAL RIVERS AND STREAMS

Route 8

Sacandaga River

Battenkill

GLOVERSVILLE

Hudson River

I-87

JOHNSTOWN

AMSTERDAM

NYSThruway

Mohawk River

Mohawk River

Hoosic River

Route 30

SCHENECTADY

I-88

I-88

ALBANY

SCHOHARIE

Schoharie Creek

MIDDLEBURGH

Map indicates
general location of
rivers and streams
discussed and
otherwise noted in
this chapter

NYSThruway

Hudson River

CHENANGO RIVER

The Chenango is Bob McNitt's river. He's lived near it, fished it, hunted it, trapped it, canoed it and loved it most of his life. He's written about it many times in his newspaper column and in the *NEW YORK SPORTSMAN* magazine. Bob introduced me to his river years ago on our first canoe-fishing trip together, and we seldom miss a year that we don't run it at least once.

I shouldn't even be writing about the Chenango River. Bob should do it, it's his river. But then again, it's my book.

Forgive me Robert, for I am about to speak of your river. Not to worry, you'll always be the stern paddler on the Chenango.

Now it would seem that after so many canoe-fishing trips on the same stream it would get boring. It would also seem that after so much publicity it would get crowded. Wrong on both counts. Every trip has been a new adventure and we seldom see other canoe-fishermen on the river.

Not that the Chenango doesn't see its share of canoes. Many individuals and groups canoe this stream, and canoe races are held here from time to time. But, keep in mind that most of the canoeists on any stream are not fishermen, and most of them like to canoe when it's warm. That leaves May, early June, September, October and early November—the best fishing months—for canoe-fishermen. Even during the summer most of the canoeing activity is on weekends, so weekday trips without competition are a good bet most of the year.

The Chenango flows south thru the hills, farmlands and swamps in central New York, through the hamlets of Eaton and Randallsville, the villages of Sherburne, Norwich, Oxford and Greene and on to the city of Binghamton where it enters the Susquehanna River. Most of the river is canoeable, but the best canoe-fishing water is north of Oxford.

Bob's favorite early season stretch is from the Middleport Rd. bridge at Randallsville off Route 12B to the Route 80 bridge at Sherburne. That's a bit long for a one-day trip—about 12 miles—but there are a number of bridges on this stretch, so shorter runs are possible and a good idea if you really want to enjoy the river and the fishing.

This stretch starts as trout water where browns up to 18 inches are not uncommon. There are a number of classic runs and riffles, ending in deep pools that hold trout, fallfish and some big suckers. On one trip, Bob and I fished these pools with lures, but didn't get a single hit or follow. When we switched to worms we caught trout at the head of the pools, suckers in the deepest areas and fallfish in the tail waters.

When the browns are in the mood for lures; spinners, spoons and plugs will take fish.

While northern pike have been abundant in downstream waters for many years, they only recently moved into upstream trout water. We discovered this migration a few years ago while fishing a once productive trout pool and caught nothing. When Bob drifted a large minnow through that pool in an attempt the catch the resident monster brown he was sure was there, a 5-pound northern ate it for lunch. On subsequent trips we caught northerns in some of the deeper pools in this area on minnows and spinners.

Trees shade much of this area of the river, keeping the water relatively cool even during the summer months, and providing habitat for a variety of wildlife. Squirrels, raccoon, muskrat, deer, ducks, herons, owls, hawks and crows are very common, as are dozens of species of song birds. While the population of raccoons and deer is usually evidenced by tracks in the mud and sand, the chances of seeing other wildlife is excellent.

As the river widens and picks up the sediments of tributaries, trout give way to walleye and smallmouth bass, and the northern pike population starts to increase. It seems that wherever there are rocks and nearby fast water, there are smallmouths, wherever there are deep holes there are walleyes, and in the weedy areas or holes near weedy areas, a few northern pike are on the prowl. Sometimes they are all in the same water.

Plastic jigs will take both bass and walleye, as will minnow imitation plugs like the Rapala. Bass also like crankbaits, spinner-jigs and spinners that look like minnows or crayfish. Pike like big spinners and spinner baits.

Walleyes go for worms, and bass like minnows and crayfish. Most of the time walleyes like their food moving slowly on the bottom of the deepest holes, while bass prefer faster moving fare in water near rocks, logs and bridge abutments. Northern pike love minnows, suspended from a bobber or lip-hooked and worked through holes and weeds. They like their artificial meat moving fast, well off the bottom, sometimes right near the surface.

Fishing is not an exact science, so it's always handing out surprises. The Chenango has provided more than it's share.

We were fishing a large hole where some floating debris had formed a line of scum next to a pile of logs, providing a canopy of shade that extended a couple of feet into the river. Bob flipped a large Mepps spinner into the scum, anticipating a strike from a bass or northern pike. Almost immediately something gobbled that lure and dove to the bottom of the hole. A few minutes later, I netted a beautiful 3-pound walleye. Go figure.

My most memorable catch was from a hole that the main current and a tributary stream had carved into the rock and gravel river bed. When my nightcrawler drifted into the bottom of that perfect walleye haven, I lifted the rod tip and started a slow retrieve. The rod tip bent to the water and my line cut across the pool. While Bob stood ready with the net, I fought that worm-eating monster as it crossed the pool several times, refusing to give up line. Bob moved the canoe over the hole and I lifted and cranked. As Bob leaned over the canoe to net my "fish" he started laughing. I had hooked and fought a **rock** to the side of the canoe. Each time I lifted it off the bottom, the current of the merging streams would push it one way and then the other. The hook had found a small indentation in the rock and held tight until I lifted it out of the net.

Don't be surprised to see flocks of ducks and Canada geese as you approach Sherburne. Rogers Environmental Conservation Center is located here and provides habitat for resident populations and resting areas for migrating waterfowl. Make every effort to visit the Center when you're in the area.

Downstream from Sherburne to Norwich is more walleye and bass water. Again there are bridges on this stretch and Route 12 parallels the river on some stretches, so shorter trips are possible and recommended. The bridge near the Hamlet of North Norwich is a good halfway point. There is an excellent access area at a park right in Norwich where Route 23 crosses the river.

The Chenango is wider in this area and tree cover is spotty, as more farms and larger communities push to the river bank. Despite the lack of continuous cover, wildlife is abundant, especially in areas near cornfields, trees and brush.

The prime northern pike water on the Chenango is from Norwich to Greene. This is relatively slow-moving water, so don't try to cover too much of the river in one run. Route 12 runs along this section of the river and there are a number of small bridges, providing plenty of places to put in and take out. As always it's a good idea to scout the river for canoe access points and parking areas.

The Chenango is one of the few rivers in the state that can be canoe-fished for over 70 miles without the worry of waterfalls, dams or rapids. The greatest dangers are piles of trees and logs, and overhanging branches during high water periods—a good time to stay off any river or stream.

WEST BRANCH FISH CREEK

The waters of Fish Creek flow off the Tug Hill Plateau and empty into Oneida Lake, creating one of the most diverse canoe-fishing streams in central New York. The cool upland waters, shaded by hardwoods and evergreen forests, provide ideal habitat for trout while the fertile waters of Oneida Lake provide a constant source of warmwater fishes. In some sections of this stream conditions are so ideal for both cold and warmwater fish, that it's always a mystery just what kind of piscatorial critter will take a lure or bait.

Fish Creek is best known for its walleye spawning runs. When conditions are right, it's loaded with walleyes when the season opens. Hundreds of anglers flock to this stream to cast jigs and plugs to mean and hungry walleyes. The rest of the year fishermen are few and far between.That's a shame because there are plenty of trout, smallmouth bass, walleye, fallfish, panfish and carp in many areas of the creek throughout the year.

Forget the East Branch of Fish Creek for canoe-fishing. It's a superb trout stream but much too rough to canoe for most of its length.

There are over 70 miles of the Chenango River to canoe-fish, and there is always the possibility that a really big fish will take your lure or bait. Bob McNitt took this walleye from a pile of logs with a Mepps spinner.

This bluff marks the junction of the East and West Branches of Fish Creek. Fish Creek is famous for its walleye runs out of Oneida Lake, but few fishermen seek the trout, smallmouth bass and walleye that live in this stream all year long.

Many central New York streams harbor some huge trout. Mark Eychner caught this 19 inch beauty from the Mohawk River near Rome by "twitching" a large floating Rapala.

Upstream reservoirs and power dams insure that West Canada Creek can be canoe-fished even during low water periods. The "Fishing Rock" near Middleville can be very productive trout and bass water as my daughter, Bridget and I discovered.

The West Branch on the other hand can be canoe-fished from Camden all the way to Oneida Lake. My favorite stretch starts at McConnellsville, and ends at the bridge near Blossvale. The canoeing is easy, there are plenty of riffles and pools, lots of shade, an absence of civilization ... **and** ... brown trout up to 20 inches, big smallmouth bass, fat walleyes, husky rock bass, fallfish up to two pounds, and carp that sometimes fight like big trout.

Stories of past adventures convinced fishing buddies Ron Gugnacki, Dave Hamilton and his son, Emlen to join me on a warm sunny day in late May. Dave and Emlen were still loading gear in their canoe when Ron and I paddled to the base of the falls in the village of McConnellsville. Ron caught a smallmouth bass on his first cast, and two others, one a 15-incher, before the rest of us could wet a line. I also hooked a bass as did Dave and Emlen. It was almost a month before bass season, so we didn't keep any fish.

I was leery of our early success. Many times in the past a terrific start meant lousy fishing the rest of the day. This was not the case on this trip. We caught a variety of fish and enjoyed a warm spring day surrounded by the sights, sounds and smells of a woodland stream.

In one hole a walleye clobbered my Mepps spinner, in another a fat, full-colored brown trout ate Ron's crayfish plug. Dave and Emlen caught bass and rockbass on plastic jigs, and refused to switch to any other lure. Fallfish ate whatever we offered.

When we beached the canoe to fish a special hole or riff, we found raccoon and deer tracks in the mud and sand. As is always the case streamside, a variety of birds greeted us along the way. There were still some spring wildflowers poking through the ferns and grasses, and the hardwoods and hemlocks that reached out and over the Creek created a tunnel through the woods.

We didn't stop long to fish the most productive waters because we had so much stream to cover in a single day. I had planned the trip to include a few extra miles so the rest of the crew could see the bluffs where the East and West branches meet.

Ron and I are impatient fishermen, so our technique was to work fast-moving lures like a spinner, spoon or plug through the best looking water and then move on. If we connected with a fish, we made a few extra casts. Dave on the other hand is patient beyond belief. He picks a hole, slowly works a plastic jig through it and then moves on. Emlen was new to this kind of fishing, so he waited for his dad to finish fishing and then helped him to catch up to us.

It was mid morning when Ron and I realized we hadn't seen Dave and Emlen for over an hour, so we stopped on a gravel bar to wait and fish. During this wait, Ron caught the biggest trout of the day, a 14-inch over-stuffed beauty that couldn't resist a tiny plug that looked like a crayfish trying to hide in a pile of logs. After I took a few photos and Ron released the fish, we started to worry.

Worry turned to wonder as a boat cushion floated around the bend. Both Dave and his son are practical jokers now and again, so we waited for them to come around the bend all smiles as we waded midstream to retrieve their life preserver. Ten minutes later they came around the bend. They were not smiling. They were very very wet.

While they were concentrating on fishing, a short rocky rapids snuck up on them. The keel on Dave's canoe hung up on the rocks. Rather than jump out of the canoe, which is a good idea when it gets hung up in shallow water, they tried to shake, paddle and rock it off. Sometimes that works, this time it didn't. The canoe rolled over. They retrieved all their gear except the cushion we picked up. The only casualty was Dave's camera. It never recovered from the dunking.

Lessons learned: If you get hung up and the water is shallow enough to stand in, it's a good idea to get out of the canoe and pull or lift it free. Cameras should be kept in watertight bags as much as possible. Same goes for wallets and other items you don't want to get wet. A canoe without a keel works best in streams because it doesn't get hung up as easily on rocks and logs.

Their experience didn't "dampen" their enjoyment of the rest of the trip, although it might have if Dave knew that his camera wouldn't recover.

The bridge at Hallstead Road near Blossvale marked the end of the "wilderness". Here camps, campgrounds and houses appeared along the stream banks. There were two consolations: except during the walleye spawning run, this area is not great fishing, and the ducks, attracted by streamside handouts, provided plenty of entertainment as we drifted through their territory. I never tire of watching puddle ducks lift off the water, fly overhead or slide to a land-

The upper reaches of the Unadilla River changes from trout and fallfish water to bass, walleye, carp and pickerel water. Here Ron Gugnacki gets Dave Hamilton to paddle from the front of the canoe while he fishes a good-looking pool off a brush-lined bank.

Schoharie Creek's abundant smallmouth bass eluded us on our fall outing, but Mark Eychner didn't mind after he caught this 4 1/2-pound walleye on a plastic jig from the waters off a sandstone shelf.

ing, so it was great fun watching the mallards and "mixed" breeds do their stuff on this lower stretch of Fish Creek.

The Creek changes dramatically when it comes out of the woods. Grasses and shrubs rather than shade trees line the banks, so the sun brightens and warms the water. The river also becomes more difficult to canoe, especially for the novice. At almost every sharp bend there are downed trees or piles of logs. In some areas the water is so fast coming into these turns that the unsuspecting canoeist can get sucked into the current and pushed into the logs.

I had warned everyone to watch out for these areas. We avoided such situations by paddling inside the turns in shallow water.

As if to prove my point, a novice kayaker got tangled up in piles of trees while we canoed through this stretch. No one was hurt, but it took 10 minutes to pry the kayak loose.

Where East meets West a high bluff dominates the scenery on the right side of the stream. It's a spectacular sight and marks the end of the West Branch of Fish Creek. Here the two branches merge to form a major feeder of Oneida Lake.

After a stop on a mid-stream island to stretch our legs, eat lunch and take some pictures, we continued downstream. Some of the big holes that held submerged trees and logs had to hold fish, but we couldn't get them to hit anything we threw at them. Live bait may have worked, but we didn't have any with us. (I learned later that a number of walleyes were taken from these big holes long after the walleye run was over.

Our adventure ended in late afternoon, just downstream from the bridge on Oswego Road where we had parked the take-out vehicles. The bank was steep, so we unloaded the canoes, hauled them up to the parking area and returned for our gear.

As we caught our collective breaths and tied the canoes to the roof racks, I looked around. Everyone was tired but smiling. We had caught fish, rubbed shoulders with mother nature, talked and laughed, and saw some beautiful country. Who could ask for more?

Most of Fish Creek is closed to ALL fishing from March 16 through the first Friday in May to protect spawning walleye. The only sections that are open are upstream from the dam at Camden on the West Branch, and upstream from the Route 69 bridge in Taberg on the East Branch.

MOHAWK RIVER

Canoe-fishing the Mohawk River is a trip through history. No other river in New York had more to do with the settlement of the state and the United States than this ribbon of water that flows west to east from the center of the state. It provided access to central New York, the Great Lakes, and ultimately to the interior of America.

Few streams have been so vital to man and so abused by man. Much of the Mohawk was so polluted by the communities and industry that developed in the Mohawk Valley that the river was "dead"—devoid of oxygen and life—by the early twentieth century. At the same time that the river was being polluted it was being altered to provide an east-west canal across the state. Today, thanks to New York's "Pure Waters" laws, the waters of the Mohawk support a variety of fish and wildlife. And, although much of the stream was swallowed up by the Erie Canal there are some stretches of the "original" Mohawk that are ideal for canoe-fishing.

Canoe-fishing water on the Mohawk starts below the dam at Delta Lake north of Rome, and runs south for six miles where it spills over a dam into the Erie Canal. There are several bridges on this stretch, so runs of a couple of hours to a full day are possible. The best takeout before the dam is at the Pinti Field across the river from the Staley Junior High School in Rome.

Very close to where the river enters the canal is the "Great Carry" that early travelers used to portage canoe and bateau from the Mohawk River to Wood Creek, thus bridging the gap between the Hudson River and the St. Lawrence River watersheds. This route, made much more convenient by the canal system, provided water access through Oneida Lake to Lake Ontario.

A couple of miles east of Rome the river and the canal separate, and except for a few short stretches the river follows its original course down the Mohawk Valley to Frankfort where it enters the canal once again. Most of the river can be canoe-fished between Rome and Frankfort. There is an abundance of wildlife in this region of the Mohawk Valley and in some areas smallmouth bass fishing can be very good. From Frankfort east the canal and river are one in the same, except for a few short stretches where they separate for a couple of miles or for a few hundred feet.

My favorite stretch of the Mohawk to canoe-fish is from below Delta dam to the bridge on the Chestnut Street entrance to Griffiss Air Force Base, just off Black River Boulevard (Route 46). This is primarily brown trout water, although walleye, northern pike, smallmouth bass and carp are also present. Each year some monster walleyes and northerns are caught below the dam.

The Rome Fish Hatchery, a major producer of trout in the state, is located near the river a mile or so below the dam. In addition to being well stocked by fish raised in the hatchery, this stretch of the Mohawk is home to some large brown trout.

Brown trout will take gold spinners, spoons, and minnow and crayfish imitation plugs. Worms are the best bait. Minnows are also a good bait for trout, and they account for some of the northern pike that are caught here each year. Plastic jigs worked through some of the deeper holes can produce an occasional walleye, trout, bass, northern ... or big carp.

Downed trees and piles of logs are the most dangerous obstacles in this area, especially during high water periods.

Almost 30 years to the day since I last canoe-fished this stretch of the Mohawk, I launched my canoe a half mile or so below Delta Dam where a dirt road and small parking area afford easy access to the River just off Route 46. With me was Mark Eychner. Mark wasn't even born when I fished these waters last, but he knows the upper Mohawk much better than I, having fished it for most of his 27 years. He has caught a number of brown trout over 18 inches from the runs and deep pools by wading the stream and casting Number 11 floating Rapalas.

"Mark, I'll handle the canoe and take the pictures. Your job is to catch one of those big browns you're always talking about", I chided as we pushed off into the current about 8:30 a.m. on the last day of May.

As we approached a soft maple that slanted over a small pool, a pair of mallards jumped from the river and flew between the branches of downstream trees. A great way to start the day.

As I guided the canoe around overhanging trees, shallow riffs, rocks, logs and small islands, Mark cast a gold Phoebe without success. When I could, I cast a gold Blue Fox spinner and managed to catch the first fish, a 10-inch brown, near the water outlet at the hatchery. Mark followed my catch with a brown that ate his Phoebe in a shallow, fast run. Right after that a smallmouth bass, hiding near a big log, tried a squirrel-tailed Mepps for breakfast. Not bad for an hour of canoe-fishing.

As we approached a long pool in which a pickup truck and an upside down car rested, I commented on how disgusting it was to see so much junk in such a beautiful stream. Mark noted that the trout didn't seem to mind because he had taken some nice fish from that hole. He promptly switched to the ultralight spinning rod with the rainbow Rapala on it.

The "junkyard" trout weren't interested in his offering that morning, but at 10 a.m. in a downstream pool, a 19-inch, 2 1\2 pound brown trout couldn't resist Mark's minnow. That "yellow" beauty went up, down, around and across that pool trying to shake loose. We had to beach the canoe to land the fish that just wouldn't give up. After some picture taking and some handshaking, Mark released it to fight another day.

The trip was more relaxing after releasing that big brown. We continued to catch fish (mostly 9 and 10-inchers on gold spinners and spoons), but we saw more of the river than riffles, runs and pools. We saw the variety of trees that lined the river bank, including hard maple, birch, elm, box elder, basswood, sycamore and willow. One huge four-clump willow must have witnessed more than a hundred years of history.

When we saw a green leafy branch floating downstream, suddenly cross the stream, we realized that a beaver was working the area.

We also shared the river with mallards, mergansers and muskrats, plus a variety of song birds.

Although the Chestnut Street Bridge is my preferred takeout, we continued downstream so I could see what the river was like in the city of Rome. It was not nice. The river bank and the river bottom in some areas looked like a junkyard. The water, however, did not seem to be polluted. In fact we caught a few trout in this area.

The school bells at Staley Junior High told us the takeout vehicle was just around the bend. We had made the entire run in 4 1/2 hours. Should have spent more time fishing the first couple of miles. Mark and I plan to do just that the next time we canoe-fish the Mohawk. Hopefully, sooner than 30 years from now.

UNADILLA RIVER

I can't say no to a canoe-fishing trip.

Ron Gugnacki, Dave Hamilton, Bob McNitt and I had planned a summer canoe-fishing trip on the Unadilla River for almost a year. Bob and I had canoe-fished the Unadilla a number of times before. We always caught fish and saw plenty of wildlife. I had bragged about these trips so many times that Dave and Ron were eager to join us on an early summer run. We would have preferred mid June for this outing, but the first week in July was the earliest we could get together. It so happened this was the hottest day of the year.

The Unadilla River flows south through farmlands and a number of small communities in central New York before it merges with the Susquehanna River near Sidney. For much of its length it's the western boundary of Otsego County. Brown trout and fallfish swim in the upper reaches of the river and it's tributaries. Further downstream the trout give way to smallmouth bass, pickerel, walleye, rock bass, and carp.

Most of this river can be canoe-fished except during periods of very high or low water. Canoeing during the spring runoff can be dangerous because of the many tree branches that hang into the water. Branches that provide welcome shade during the summer can sweep a canoe clean or gobble it up when runoff water is five feet above normal. Downed trees and logs that pile up at bends in the river can also be hazardous when the river is rampaging. During low water periods the upper reaches of the Unadilla are too low to float a canoe, so the best time to canoe-fish this part of the river is in May and June. The lower reaches, below South Edmeston, are more productive in May and June, and in the fall, but can be canoe-fished throughout the summer.

In addition to the bridges in the towns and villages, there are a number of small bridges along the river where canoe access is possible. Unfortunately a number of these bridges are closed, so it's not possible to cross the river on some roads. Scouting the roads, bridges and stream from your car, using county road maps or a DeLorme "New York State Atlas & Gazetteer" as a guide, is a good idea. Access areas change from time to time, as we learned on this trip.

Because we had to make our trip on the hottest day in July, Bob picked a stretch of the river that was well shaded, so the predicted bright sun and mid 90's temperatures had less impact on fish and fishermen. His plan was to launch the canoes just south of the village of New Berlin and take out at South New Berlin, an area where we expected to catch smallmouths, walleyes and some big rock-bass.

Those best laid plans were trashed by a disgruntled farmer who had put a gate across the dirt road that led to the launch site. The gate was locked and we didn't have time to track down the gate keeper, so Bob hastily made a new plan.

"This won't be as good fishing, and we'll have to walk the canoes through some areas, but we should get into fish and see some wildlife.", Bob explained as we unloaded the canoes at the first bridge above South Edmeston. The sun was already bright and hot.

Everyone but me was dressed for a summer outing with short sleeve shirts, shorts, sneakers and ball caps. I looked out of place with my long sleeved shirt, long pants and canvas hat, but I sunburn easily and hate the heat of summer.

It felt great to finally get out of the vehicles and into our canoes. Bob and I pushed off in his Grumman aluminum canoe while Dave and Ron launched my Mad River Explorer. As predicted we had to walk the canoes through several riffles, and except for a few fall-fish we didn't really get into fish until we were well downstream. No problem. There was plenty of entertainment.

At first ducks, great blue heron, muskrats, woodchucks, deer tracks and beaver slides kept our attention. Then we heard a "gong" upstream ... and the real entertainment began. The first aluminum canoe rounded the bend, bounced off a rock, turned 180 degrees in midstream and zipped through a short riffle. The young occupants were having a ball. Four more canoes followed, all but one with young teenagers learning how **not** to negotiate the river. Their instructor and guide, a young lady from Rogers Environmental Conservation Center in nearby Sherburne, joined us in laughter as her students bounced their way downstream. We stopped for lunch so they could get out of sight and sound before we resumed fishing.

While we stood on a gravel bar eating sandwiches and downing cold drinks, I realized how comfortable I was despite the heat of the midday sun that we learned later was 93 in the shade. My canvas hat and the legs of my long pants were soaked, providing air conditioning from top to bottom. I noticed a tinge of red on the legs of my compadres.

After lunch we switched partners ... and started catching fish. Actually Bob and Dave started catching fish. Somehow they managed to stay just ahead of Ron and me, taking fish from the limited deep and shaded water. Ron and I managed to catch a few small smallmouth bass and some fallfish, but it was no contest as the leading canoe caught pickerel and some large smallmouth bass.

Catching the variety of fish that swim in the Unadilla requires a variety of techniques. In the upstream trout waters, worms and spinners will take fish from pools, runs and from the holes near logs and rocks. The smallmouth bass that take over for trout further downstream like live crayfish, crayfish and minnow imitations, plastic jigs and spinners. They hang out close to rocks and logs, bridge abutments and in pools just below fast water. Rockbass are often found with smallmouths and they like the same lures, plus worms.

As the river picks up water and sediments from tributaries, it creates walleye water—deep holes of turbid water, often filled with roots and logs. Plastic jigs, purple is especially effective, plus worms and minnows will take fish from the bottom of these holes when worked slowly.

Pickerel like weeds, so the best place to fish for them is in or near small weedy bays, backsets and stream outlets. They love minnows, but spinners, spoons and plastic jigs will also take these eating machines.

Fallfish will take anything a trout or bass will, including flies. They are often found in fast water, but prefer the quiet water of holes, pools, eddies and small bays. Carp like mud and weeds, and can be caught on worms, corn, doughballs and plastic jigs.

The best fish of the day were two hefty smallmouths caught by Bob and Dave near the takeout bridge at South Edmeston. Both fish fell for plastic jigs bounced off the bottom; one near a log jam and the other next to a bridge abutment. Ron and I arrived on the scene just in time to see Bob's fish dancing on the water.

While Ron and Bob went for our upstream vehicle, Dave and I carried the canoes and gear up to the road. The heat of the day had taken it's toll. Everyone but me had sunburned legs. We were all hot, tired and glad the trip was over.

This was not our best ever canoe-fishing trip. It was too hot for man or beast, there were few trees to shade the river, and the water was too low for good canoeing or good fishing.

Would I make the trip again? In a minute. Even the bad ones are great fun. That's why I can't say no to a canoe-fishing trip.

SUSQUEHANNA RIVER

Canoe-fishing is a funny business. Sometimes everything goes just right and sometimes it goes all wrong. It seemed to be going all wrong when Bob McNitt and I started our trip on the Susquehanna River one bright sunny day late in the summer.

Neither of us had canoed this water but Bob had fished it years ago by wading stretches near the streamside communities of Otego and Wells Bridge. He remembered catching some nice smallmouth bass from riffles, runs and pools, and he had talked to area anglers who had connected with some good walleyes and an occasional muskie. Sounded like the kind of water we like to canoe-fish.

And it looked like the water we like to canoe-fish at Wells Bridge where we parked my Jeep for the takeout. Downstream from the bridge we could see a series of riffles, runs and pools that just reeked of smallmouth bass. Upstream two canoe-fishermen were casting the rocky shore of a stretch of flatwater. Looking good.

We drove Route 7 upstream to Otego expecting to launch at one of the bridges that cross the river. The bridge at the main crossroad in town was down, apparently due to the construction of Interstate 88. The river of course was there, but the land was well posted, so we stopped at a nearby Agway store to ask where we could launch the canoe. We were directed to a State launch on the other side of the river that was some two miles downstream. Things were not going well.

We went back to the Route 88 exit for Otego, crossed the river and drove downstream on the Wells Bridge - Otego Road to a well maintained hand-launch. We could have reached this launch in 10 minutes by crossing at Wells Bridge where we left the takeout vehicle. We had wasted over an hour of good fishing time, and the flatwater at the launch site was disappointing.

Heh, it was a nice day and Bob and I hadn't canoe-fished together all summer. We had a lot to catch up on and the river beckoned.

"Sorry about this Paul. I was sure we could launch at Otego. Should have scouted this trip better", Bob said as he cast a Mepps spinner at a fallen tree. "I don't like this kind of water. Tough to find fish."

"There's better water ahead. We'll just have to cast to shoreline rocks and downed trees, and paddle through the rest until we get to our kind of water", I explained needlessly.

As if to point the way a great blue heron lifted off a dead tree and flew down the middle of the river. For an hour or so we followed that heron and cast spinners and crankbaits to any structure we could see. We didn't connect with a single fish.

We continued our pursuit until we met the two canoe-fishermen who had launched at Wells Bridge and fished upstream. They were casting minnow-type plugs along a rocky shoreline. Although they fished this stretch of flatwater a couple of times a week and usually did well on smallmouths they hadn't caught a fish all morning. That was enough for us. We reeled in and headed for the downstream riffles, runs and pools even if they were below our takeout vehicle.

As we settled in for the mile or so paddle, we scanned the river and the shoreline for wildlife. A small flock of mergansers resting on a gravel bar fanned their wings and then wing-skipped down the river when we got too close. A kingfisher flew by without giving us a customary scolding. Beaver runs led from nearby fields to floating cornstalks. Huge tent caterpillar nests covered the branches of some shagbark hickory trees, while adjacent willows and maples were left unscathed.

My first cast with a gold Blue Fox spinner into the fast water near the bridge produced a smallmouth bass that took to the air. Things were looking up. This was definitely our kind of water— long riffles, leading to rock-strewn runs that ended in deep pools that led to more riffles, runs and pools. For the next hour and a half we caught fish on spinners, plugs and spinner-jigs. Most of the fish were smallmouths, but a few were rockbass, fallfish and walleye.

We had to pole and paddle hard to get back to the bridge and our takeout vehicle but it was worth it. We could have walked the canoe back but didn't feel like getting wet.

We left the river that day having re-learned a valuable lesson. Scouting a stream you haven't canoed or fished in a long time is a very good idea. The stream itself might not change much over the years, but access to that stream can change dramatically. In this case the construction of an interstate highway had closed off a number of bridges and other areas where a canoe could be easily and legally launched. In this case we were led further astray by the fact that the road map we were using indicated that the bridge at Otego was still in service.

We knew that the Susquehanna was canoeable for most of its length, and that resident smallmouths and walleyes could provide plenty of action. We wanted to canoe-fish a 5–6 mile stretch in the upper reaches of the river where there was some moderately moving water that would provide good fish habitat and carry the canoe downstream while we caught fish. The Otego to Wells Bridge section seemed ideal. On the day we tried it wasn't. Of course had we caught fish in all that flatwater the story would have been different.

The next time we canoe-fish the Susquehanna, we'll put in at Wells Bridge and take out at the village of Unadilla. It's a longer run —about seven miles—but it starts with our kind of water. A subsequent drive to this area revealed that we could have launched on the other side of the old Otego crossing by driving upstream on the old road that runs along the south side of the river. However, streamside observation and talking to a canoe-fisherman confirmed that the run from Wells Bridge to Unadilla is the best stretch in the area for smallmouth bass. There are takeout points along Route 7 upstream of the village of Unadilla, and a State hand-launch on the other side of the river (reached from the I-88 exit road) downstream of the village. This follow-up scouting trip also revealed that the Unadilla Diner on Route 7 is the place to stop for breakfast and homemade soups and pies.

WEST CANADA CREEK

It looks like a river to me, so that's what I call it most of the time. But, no matter what you call it, this clearwater Adirondack stream becomes prime canoe-fishing water when it gushes from the Trenton Gorge at the village of Trenton Falls.

The West Canada in this area can be fished all the way to the Mohawk River at Herkimer, but the longest continuous run of easy-water canoe-fishing (no bad rapids, dams or falls) is from Trenton Falls to the fishermen's parking area just downstream from the village of Poland. (Don't be fooled by the calm water here; just around the bend are "expert canoeist" rapids, especially during high water.)

Another good stretch of canoe-fishing water is from Newport to Middleville. There is plenty of fast water in this area, but unless the water is low, it's easy to canoe. If the water is low, plan to walk the canoe through some areas. You can launch just below the bridge and power plant at Newport and take out on the south side of the river just upstream from Middleville.

There are a number of bridges and roadside parking areas on the West Canada, so it's easy to plan a trip for as little as an hour or up to a full day. The first 2.5 miles are Special Trout Waters where only lures can be used to take fish and the limit and size are restricted to three fish over 12 inches. Below the outlet of Cincinnati Creek, you can use bait as well as lures.

Most anglers seek brown trout that run up to 20 inches, but a 12-inch fish is considered a good catch. The state stocks the West Canada quite heavily with browns each spring. Brook trout are not stocked by the state but there is some natural production of brookies in small tributary streams. Occasionally they are caught near the mouths of these streams.

Fallfish (up to 3 pounds) will take anything that a trout will and they're usually in the same locations. They hit hard but give up after a short battle.

There are smallmouth bass in every area of the creek below Trenton Falls, especially near deep pools, small bays, large rocks and submerged trees. Their size and numbers increase in the lower, slow water sections near the village of Poland.

All of these fish will take a floating Rapala minnow, a Rebel crayfish plug, a Mepps or Panther Martin spinner, a Phoebe, a small plastic jig, and just about any other lure that works for you in other streams. Carry a variety of colors.

Mark Eychner almost always fishes a Number 9, floating Rapala and he made no exception to that rule when we fished the West Canada. For the first half hour he didn't catch a single fish, while I had a number of hits and caught a trout and a fallfish on a silver bladed Panther Martin spinner. I suggested he change color from gold to silver. From then on he caught two fish to my one, including a 2 1/2 pound smallmouth. On a subsequent trip with his brother Gary, Mark caught a 20-inch brown trout on that same plug.

When Bob McNitt and I fished this stream during the heat of summer, he caught trout, bass and fallfish on a tiny shimmy shad plastic jig. Other anglers have done the same by fishing their favorite lures.

Where you put your lure and how you retrieve it has as much to do with fishing success as the type of offering. Both Mark and Bob put their lures right where the fish were waiting for dinner, and retrieved it the way a minnow swims when it's hurt. Mark twitched the rod tip as he retrieved his Rapala, and Bob swam the shimmy shad by raising and lowering his rod tip.

Most of the fish in the West Canada wait for dinner just out of the current, near islands, bridge abutments, rocks, logs, eddies and small bays. There are many deep, fast runs in this stream, usually along one bank, but sometimes in midstream, that hold some good fish. The undercut banks and underwater rocks that are invisible to anglers provide calm-water pockets for feeding fish.

In some areas the West Canada has carved long, narrow pools downstream from large rocks and midstream bridge abutments. These pools are difficult to fish from shore, but not from a canoe. Years ago a fishing buddy and I took our limits of brown trout from one of these pools below an old bridge abutment while shoreline anglers couldn't catch a fish. I can usually depend on this pool to yield a couple of trout. A 50-foot long pool below one large rock is always good for a smallmouth bass.

Casting a lure into these areas as you drift by will often produce fish, but to really work this water, it's a good idea to anchor the canoe upstream or to one side.

West Canada water is usually cool because it flows from the bottom of upstream dams, but during the heat of summer, cast to shade because that's where the fish are, especially trout. Again, the shoreline angler has a tough time reaching these spots, but from a canoe, it's easy.

This section of the West Canada can be canoe-fished even during low water periods because water is released from upstream power dams around 9 a.m.. Canoe-fisherman have a couple of hours to launch during this release and ride it all day. This rising water reaches the village of Poland around noon. Many canoeists make the mistake of thinking the water is high everywhere on the stream at the same time. I've heard a number of them complaining about bottoming out in their canoes because they launched before or after the water-release passed through their section of the stream. Incidentally, the fish get turned on by this rising water.

If you wade this stream or beach your canoe before the water rises, be prepared. You can get into big trouble if you're in midstream or your canoe isn't tied up.

Part of the joy of canoe-fishing is seeing wildlife, and the West Canada attracts more than its share. There are respectable populations of merganser and mallard ducks, Canada geese, great blue heron and osprey that feed on or near the river. Other wildlife that you are likely to see are wood ducks, owls, crows, kingfisher, muskrat, whitetail deer, squirrels and a variety of songbirds.

For information on accommodations and attractions write to: Leatherstocking Country, 327 N. Main St., PO Box 447, Herkimer, NY 13350.

SCHOHARIE CREEK

I've never canoe-fished a stream that I knew so little about. The only information I had about upper Schoharie Creek was that it could be canoed between Middleburgh and Schoharie and that it was smallmouth bass water. When Mark Eychner and I launched the canoe below Middleburgh on the first Sunday in October, we had no idea how many surprises were waiting for us.

After parking the takeout vehicle near the Bridge Street bridge just off Route 30 in the village of Schoharie, we drove to Middleburgh, turned right on Route 145, crossed the river and drove downstream about a half mile to a dirt road that offers access to the water. It was 50 degrees, windy, but sunny, not a hint of rain. We had found a place to put in and a place to take out about seven miles apart. So far so good.

When we pushed out into the current three sandpipers flying upstream in close formation seemed intent on strafing the canoe, but veered at the last moment. First time I ever started a canoe trip with a flyover. Around the first bend a great blue heron, that was to become our constant companion, stood proudly in shallow water, . lifting off only when we were close enough to see his eyeballs. Just downstream from the heron were a dozen domestic geese sitting on a small island. They honked when we went by but didn't budge. Mergansers left the water soon after we passed the geese and flew downriver.

It looked great for smallmouths; long riffles leading to pools and runs, mostly over a rock and gravel streambed. In many areas the fast water was so low we had to walk the canoe through, so it seemed that the smallmouths would concentrate in the runs and pools. Everything looked right, but we couldn't get a single fish to bite. After more than three hours we were convinced the bass had moved to deeper downstream water, so we decided to paddle through, casting only to the best looking spots.

With "great blue" leading the way, we covered water, looking for a very deep pool or run near a rock ledge. I had caught fish in similar water in other streams. We found several outcrops but none with water more than a couple feet deep.

Most of the stream bank was lined with willows, soft maple, basswood and cottonwood, a few sycamore and some trees I had never seen before. I first noticed this strange tree by the fruit floating in the river. When I found a concentration of these green apple-like balls near a large tree, I gave it the once over. My tree identification book indicates they are Osage-orange or "hedge apple" trees that originated in the southwestern United States and were widely planted and became naturalized in the East.

In some areas cornfields grew just inside the tree line. From time to time we could hear gunshots as bird hunters worked these fields. Beaver had also taken advantage of the corn, dragging stalks to the river over well-worn slides. The "larder" next to a large beaver house was almost entirely cornstalks. Not far from the beaver house was another surprise.

Schoharie Creek is no small stream. It's bigger water than most rivers in the state. Fact is until around 1800 it was called the Schoharie River. In any case it's not the kind of water where you'd expect to see a beaver dam. Yet, there it was, two-feet high and a good 50-feet long. First time I'd seen so many cornstalks in a beaver dam.

Just below the beaver dam were the remains of an old earthen dam that had been made by dumping rocks and gravel between pilings. Next to this manmade pile of rocks was a deep hole. Not quite what we were looking for, but we worked it with spinners and plugs. Not even a snag.

Mark caught a fallfish on a Rapala from a long run that should have held a couple of bass. As we drifted out of this run into shallow water and had to walk, Mark scooped up a crayfish and dropped it in a puddle of water in the canoe.

We were hungry and tired when we finally came to a long deep pool next to a rock outcrop where the water was at least five feet deep, the deepest water we had seen since the beginning of our trip. Hunger outweighed my eagerness to fish, so I opened the cooler and spread sandwiches and drink on a large flat rock. Mark rigged up the crayfish and tossed it into the hole, propping the rod in the canoe. Before he got two bites out of his sandwich, the rod took a tumble and Mark ran back to the canoe. No fish on. Another try produced a few nibbles, but no fish. A rock ledge finally snagged the bait.

After lunch, I tied on a chartreuse plastic jig and cast it to the middle of the river. A fish took it on the first hop off the bottom. It was a 9-inch perch. Two casts later a bigger fish ate the jig. It was an 18-inch walleye.

Faster than a speeding bullet Mark had a chartreuse plastic jig on his rod and was casting into the pool about 50-feet upstream. His first fish was a 13-inch smallmouth. There really were smallies in the Schoharie. His second fish was a big fallfish.

After a half hour of no fish and losing jigs to the underwater rock ledge, we decided to move on. On his way back to the canoe Mark made a couple casts. As he worked the jig from midstream to the edge of the ledge, a fish took it and held on. Mark's rod tip bent to the river. The following conversation ensued.

MARK: "It feels like a big smallmouth."

PAUL: "Fights like a walleye."

MARK: "It's a walleye. The biggest walleye I've ever caught in ... my ... life!"

That walleye was 24 inches long and weighed 4 1\2 pounds. Suddenly a good canoe-fishing trip became a great canoe-fishing trip. I took a dozen pictures of Mark's fish before we returned to the canoe.

We had been on the river for about 4 1\2 hours and didn't know how far it was to the takeout. We paddled hard, reaching the Bridge at Schoharie in less than an hour. After fishing the deep water near the bridge for a few minutes, we hauled the canoe and gear up the steep trail to Mark's car.

In this case knowing almost nothing about the river was a boon. We found something new at every bend, met friendly "wildlife", saw a tree I had never seen before, crossed a beaver dam where there shouldn't be one, and caught a big walleye in a river noted for smallmouth bass. Never did find those bass. Maybe next time.

TIOUGHNIOGA RIVER

I waited a long time to canoe-fish the Tioughnioga (tee-off-nee-oga) River. I had heard that a few stream fishermen in the know consistently took trout from the upper reaches, caught some nice smallmouths and walleyes from Cortland downstream, and occasionally latched onto some big walleyes, northern pike and tiger muskies all the way from Truxton to Chenango Bridge. I had also read that much of this stream was popular among central New York canoeists. Typically, hardly anyone canoed-fished the river.

I had also waited a long time to fish with J. Michael Kelly. In addition to being the outdoor writer for the Syracuse Post-Standard, he has written—and received awards—for magazine articles about fishing and hunting in New York State. I was particularly impressed with his fishing articles, so when I learned that he had canoe-fished the Tioughnioga a number of times, I asked him to show me where and how. He agreed to join me on the river in mid-October.

Unfortunately, we couldn't canoe Mike's favorite stretch from Blodgett Mills to Marathon because the water was so low, so we decided on a half-day run below Whitney Point. After leaving Mike's car beside the road just above the abandoned bridge at Itaska, we drove up Route 79 to launch the canoe near the Whitney Point bridge. It was 9 a.m, 37 degrees and the sun was starting to burn off the fog that hung over the river.

Two young boys were casting into the waters near the bridge. As we pushed the canoe from shore, a sea gull flew downstream, carrying a good-size fish. At the first bend we spooked a great blue heron and a dozen mergansers. Good signs perhaps.

Mike started casting a floating perch Rapala almost immediately. He had taken bass, northern pike and walleye on this same lure when he canoe-fished his favorite upstream run. His biggest walleye was 27 inches long and weighed nearly six pounds. I rigged my ultralight with a gold Blue Fox spinner that had taken a number of bass and walleyes throughout the year.

The Tioughnioga is bordered by farmland in this area and the river banks are lined with silver maples, willows and some of the biggest Sycamore trees I've seen in New York. I was surprised to see apple trees growing near the river—not common on most streams I've canoe-fished.

The river runs from riffle to pool, riffle to pool over a rocky bottom. Although we expected to find fish in the deeper pools at this time of year, we also cast to faster water on occasion. Mike's lure was bumped a couple of times, but nothing held on for the first hour or so. My spinner connected with a good-size fish in a deep swirling hole. It took a minute or so to get that fish off the bottom and to the side of the canoe, but I lost it. I guessed it to be a 2–3 pound walleye. Mike switched to a Panther Martin spinner.

Fisheries Biologist, Dave Lemon of the DEC office in Cortland told me that their tagging studies indicate that the walleyes in the Susquehanna River watershed are very migratory, traveling up to a hundred miles during the year. Some of these walleyes move up the Tioughnioga after spawning in the Susquehanna. A fisherman took a big walleye near Truxton that summer that was tagged in the Binghamton area during the spring spawning season. Dave noted that 10-pound walleyes are not uncommon in the Tioughnioga.

We didn't catch any big walleyes, tigers, northerns or bass on that cold October morning. Mike's Panther Martin spinner did entice a big fallfish from a big pool, and as the sun warmed the water, we saw some big carp. Other than that our outing was fishless.

The highlight of the trip was the growing flock of mergansers we pushed downstream. It started with a dozen at the launch site and grew to more than 40 birds when we reached the takeout. The sight of all those ducks lifting off the river was very impressive.

We also saw a number of wood ducks, some crows, kingfisher, great blue heron and a redtailed hawk. Unlike the mergansers, the woodies flew overhead and returned to upstream feeding areas.

Canoeing was a snap on this stretch of the river, although in a few areas we had to walk through low water. Mike noted that the longer upstream run he preferred to canoe-fish earlier in the year was also easy to canoe, except perhaps during the spring runoff.

When we beached the canoe at the takeout around noon, I wished we had more time to spend on the river. There had to be some monster walleyes in some of those downstream pools. Heh, there's always next year.

OTHER CENTRAL RIVERS AND STREAMS TO CANOE-FISH

BATTENKILL
HOOSIC RIVER
OTSELIC RIVER

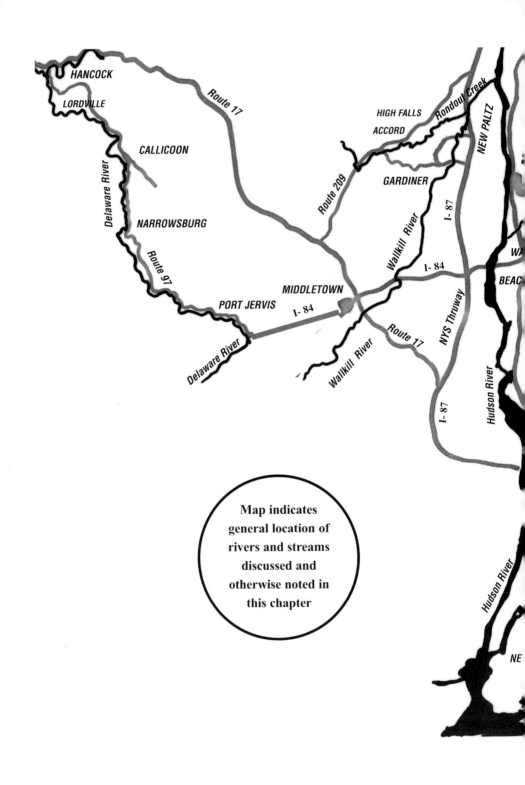

HANCOCK

LORDVILLE

CALLICOON

NARROWSBURG

Delaware River

Route 17

Route 97

PORT JERVIS

Delaware River

MIDDLETOWN

I- 84

I- 84

Wallkill River

Route 17

HIGH FALLS

ACCORD

Rondout Creek

NEW PALTZ

GARDINER

I- 87

Route 209

Wallkill River

NYS Thruway

BEAC

WA

Hudson River

I- 87

Hudson River

NE

Map indicates
general location of
rivers and streams
discussed and
otherwise noted in
this chapter

CHAPTER 11

SOUTHERN RIVERS AND STREAMS

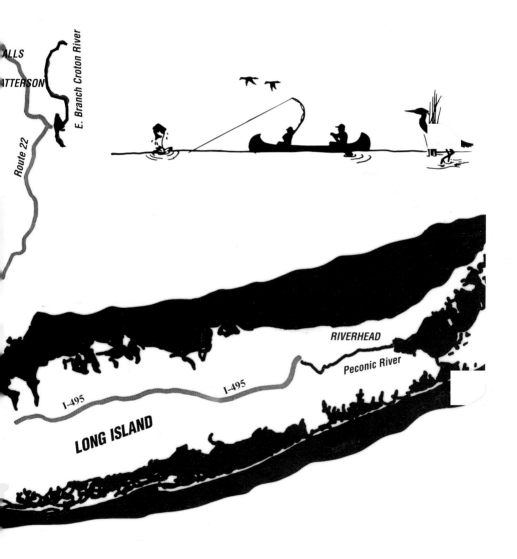

WALLKILL RIVER

Ron Gugnacki and I have fished and canoed together for some 25 years. Most of our outings have been on the rivers and streams in upstate New York, so a trip to the southern part of the state was an adventure and a challenge for us. We had to locate streams that would qualify as easy-water for canoeing, offer ready access, provide reasonably good fishing and, hopefully, the chance to see wildlife. Then we had to locate launch and takeout points, and figure out how to do it all with only one vehicle.

The good folks at the DEC office in New Paltz pointed us in the direction of the Wallkill River and Rondout Creek. Both streams were canoeable and there were good populations of smallmouth bass, rockbass and carp. There was also a developing walleye fishery in the Wallkill and some trout water in the upper area of the Rondout.

We had one problem. The only time we could make these runs was in May. Unfortunately bass season doesn't start until the third Saturday in June, so we couldn't legally fish for bass. We solved that problem by fishing for rockbass, walleyes and trout. We would probably catch smallmouth bass, but wouldn't keep any fish, or use bait or lures to specifically catch bass. I know that sounds like a game, but it was the only way we could legally fish these streams when the water was certain to be high enough to canoe. An added bonus was that wildlife is especially active in the spring.

So, with access sites marked on our road maps, we made plans for two days of canoe-fishing.

The seven mile stretch of the Wallkill we planned to run started at a small tributary just east of the village of Gardiner (off Route 9) and ended at the New Paltz Boat Launch, south of the Route 299 bridge on the west side of the river. DEC Fisheries Biologist, Bob Angyal solved our one-vehicle situation by returning me to the launch site after I parked my vehicle at the takeout. As we drove upstream on Route 7, which parallels much of this section of the river, Bob pointed out some good stretches of water.

It was noon when Ron and I worked our way through creek boulders, passed under a small bridge, drifted by a private campground and caught the main current of the Wallkill River. Suddenly the long drive from home, the hubbub of New Paltz traffic and getting setup on unfamiliar water, faded from memory as two pairs of mallards lifted from the river and flew downstream under a canopy of soft maples and oak trees.

More mallards and some wood ducks flew downriver as we cast spinners, tiny plugs and plastic jigs to rocks, downed trees and into pools and riffs. We didn't catch a fish for almost an hour. At the inside of a long sweeping bend in the river, I cast a Panther Martin into the quiet water below a riff. The lure stopped and my ultralight spinning rod bent almost double.

"I've got a snag. Let's go back", I instructed.

Ron grabbed his paddle and turned the canoe around to save my lure. When we were almost even with the "snag" it moved upstream. A big fish was at the end of the line. It felt like a swimming log. When it turned downstream and moved into the current my pencil thin rod bent to the water. The reel drag wouldn't give up line, so I tried to adjust it with the fish on. A big mistake. The loosened drag gave up line just as the fish cut cross current. The line went slack and the fish was gone. I never saw that fish, but I'd like to think it was a huge walleye.

More likely it was a huge carp, because while I was fighting that mystery monster, an angler fishing from shore on the other side of the river was fighting a big carp. He was fishing with what looked to be a 10-12 foot surfcasting rod. A large long-handled net lay on the river bank. When we paddled over to watch him land his fish, his second that afternoon, he explained, with a strong East European accent, that he only fishes for carp and his only bait is worms. This was his favorite spot.

As we worked our way down the Wallkill, the Shawangunk Mountains came into view. The clouded blue sky, spring-green colors of new leaves, and the black and white mountain ledges provided one of the most spectacular sights I've seen while canoe-fishing in New York State. I'm certain local residents take it for granted.

After latching on to that big fish in deep water, we concentrated our efforts in that direction. Ron fished a curly tailed plastic jig while I cast a tiny crayfish plug. We caught several smallmouth bass in the 13 - 15 inch range. Proof positive that there is a healthy population of smallies in the Wallkill.

There was also a healthy population of wildlife. In addition to the ducks mentioned earlier, we saw Canada geese, osprey, turkey vultures, orioles, killdeer, a crow being attacked by a dozen black-birds, and a great blue heron carrying a stick, for a nest no doubt.

There is only one short rapids. We got through this "boulder field" without a problem, but they could be dangerous during high or very low water. If in doubt get out and walk around. You can see this area from Route 7 at Libertyville.

We didn't catch a single walleye, although we saw a number of signs asking for information on walleyes caught from the river. DEC and local sportsmen organizations are working together to develop this fishery by stocking walleyes and monitoring angler success.

The last couple of miles was flatwater, so we paddled most of the time. The steel bridge at New Paltz was a welcome sight. It had been a long day and our takeout was just downstream. We were tired, hungry and in need of a shower.

Two hours later: clean, rested and fed, we were excited about fishing Rondout Creek the next day.

RONDOUT CREEK

When DEC Fisheries Biologist, Bob Angyal mentioned the Rondout and trout in the same breath, Ron Gugnacki's face lit up. I knew I wouldn't have to talk him into canoe-fishing this Catskill Mountain stream. The thought of a heavy brown trout at the business end of his spinning rod was all the encouragement he needed.

Bob had explained that while most of the good trout water on the Rondout was not canoeable, the upper reaches of the canoeable stretch between the villages of Accord and High Falls held some good trout, especially near the mouths of tributary streams. He also noted that the most populous fish in this stretch of the Rondout was smallmouth bass and rockbass. Rockbass are always in season, but bass season didn't open until the third weekend in June.

Ron and I live upstate and didn't want to drive two vehicles, so we rented a "well used car" in New Paltz for our takeout vehicle. At 7:30 a.m. on a clear, cool morning in early May, we drove both vehicles west on Route 6, over the Shawangunk Mountains, past Mohonk, down to Route 6A and north to High Falls. We left the rental car at a small roadside parking area a mile or so upstream from the village, on the west side of the creek, and drove to Accord. At 8:20 we launched the canoe on Rochester Creek and drifted into the swirling waters of the Rondout. This was to be one of our most memorable canoe-fishing adventures.

The water near the mouth of Rochester Creek smelled of trout. We cast spinners and plugs into deep runs, fast water and holes filled with downed trees and piles of logs. I cranked hard on a large floating Rapala to work it through the head of a pool. It stopped. I could feel a big fishing shaking the lure at the bottom of the pool. When Ron heard the reel drag he grabbed his paddle to turn the canoe around, but it was too late. The fish was gone.

We continued to fish hard in that trout water for more than an hour but couldn't connect with another fish. So, as always when the fish are not cooperative, we settled down and looked around, casting now and then to especially inviting water.

Soft maple, sycamore, beech and willows leaned over the water. The morning sun illuminated pastel green leaves that contrasted beautifully with a deep blue sky. A large hawk soared high over the scene. Three turkey vultures did the same but at a lower altitude. As we drifted around a bend, four Canada geese lifted from the creek, feet and wingtips dripping water. What a magnificent sight. We held our breath and fumbled for cameras. We saw a dozen pair of geese on the Rondout that day, and lost count of the mallards and mergansers.

A couple miles downstream the Rondout slowly changed from a lowland valley stream to a mountain stream. Tree lined dirt and sand banks became tree lined rocky outcrops where hemlock and white pine mixed with hardwoods. Midstream rocks were more common in this area. It reminded me of similar waters in the Adirondacks.

We heard it before we saw it. Sounded like rapids. No one had mentioned a rapids, but there it was stretched before us, a good quarter mile of water running fast over acres of boulders. It didn't take long to realize we couldn't paddle through them. Two choices: portage around or walk the canoe through. We picked the latter. Wrong choice.

The rocks were covered with dead, grey, teflon-slick algae. At first we both tried to walk with the canoe, but after 15 minutes of slipping and sliding in opposite directions, Ron volunteered to handle the canoe while I took pictures. Sounded like a good plan to me.

It took us a half hour to get through the rapids and finally paddle under the Alligerville Bridge. Had we scouted this run a little better we would have seen the rapids from the bridge. Considering their length and slick bottom, a portage is best. Alligerville is also a good place to end a half-day trip.

Despite the beauty of the river and the abundance of wildlife, we continued to fish. Ron, as is often the case, caught most of the fish. His plastic jig enticed rockbass, fallfish and a few smallmouths from the deep holes near rocky outcrops. After going fishless for so long, I switched to a curly tailed jig and managed to boat a couple of rock bass.

We stopped for lunch at a huge outcrop that Ron dubbed fossil rock. This area had been an inland sea eons ago and supported a variety of critters that became embedded in the sea floor. Over millions of years the sea floor had turned to solid rock. Upheavals and erosion had exposed outcrops of this rock along the Rondout, providing cover for fish and places to stop for lunch.

We saw more Canada geese, dozens of ducks, hawks, turkey vultures, sandpiper, muskrat, grey squirrels and turtles between Alligerville and High Falls. When I commented on all the wildlife we were seeing, Ron noted we hadn't seen a deer. Almost on cue a small whitetail buck appeared high on the stream bank. That little fellow entertained us for a good ten minutes before disappearing into the underbrush. We had already seen more wildlife on the Rondout than we had on any other stream in New York. And it wasn't over yet.

A white blob floated on the water near the upper end of an island. From a distance it looked like a large plastic barrel or jug, but quickly took the form of a mute swan. As we drew closer the huge bird pulled its long neck back and tucked its head into the feathers on its back. We took a few photographs and moved on to our take-out vehicle. It was 2 p.m. when we pulled the canoe from the water.

This area of the Rondout is noted for smallmouth bass. True we weren't targeting smallmouths because the season wasn't open and the water was too cold, but the same lures that take trout, rockbass and fallfish should have enticed a bass now and then. Except for a few puny specimens, that didn't happen to us. Just as well. I don't know if we could have handled good fishing and all the wildlife we saw. Without a doubt, that day on the Rondout was one of our most memorable canoe-fishing adventures.

DELAWARE RIVER

Two feet of silver launched at the surface, arched over the river and dove for the bottom. All I could do was keep the rod tip high, hold on ... and scream like a banshee.

"It's coming up again. Will you look at that fish go?", I yelled as the fish repeated its performance again and again. I was so excited I could hardly sit still in the canoe. My partner had no such compunction. Suddenly the canoe started tipping from side to side. Bob McNitt, camera in hand, was standing up in the back of the canoe trying to get a photograph of my jumping fish.

"Bob will you sit down. If you tip us over and I lose this fish, you'll be in big trouble", I pleaded. At the time the thought of dumping our fishing gear and cameras didn't enter my mind.

The Delaware River from Hancock to Port Jervis is a canoe-fisherman's dream ... almost. There are no dams, no significant rapids, plenty of access points ... and fish top to bottom. I had wanted to canoe-fish this NewYork-Pennsylvania border-water for years, but never had the opportunity—or motivation—until I started working on this book. After trying unsuccessfully to find someone who had canoed **and** fished the river, I asked some canoe-fishing buddies to join me on the Delaware in late May.

In mid-May my wife and I scouted the river to locate two, 5–6-mile runs where the canoeing was easy and the fishing could be exciting and different. After spending most of a day driving up and down the river between Hancock and Narrowsburg; talking to park rangers, tackle store owners, canoeists and fishermen, and looking at the river at every crossover, I decided on two stretches some 30 miles apart. The lower section was from Narrowsburg to the mouth of Ten Mile River. Access is exceptional at both ends with public launch areas and plenty of parking. There are small-mouth bass, walleye, panfish and carp in this warmer section of river throughout the year, and American shad are in the river during the month of May.

The biggest drawback to canoe-fishing this area during the warmer months, especially on weekends and in the summer, are wall to wall canoes. Canoeing is big business here. Canoe liveries rent hundreds of canoes to enthusiasts from metropolitan New York and New Jersey. So, our trip had to be in May while shad were in the river and during the week when the canoeing flotilla was ashore.

The upstream run was more difficult to plan. I wanted five miles of trout water, which meant somewhere between Hancock and Long Eddy. Problem was that during the spring months the upper reaches of this area of the Delaware are popular with fly fishing guides who float the river in dories and rubber rafts. So, I decided to launch well below Hancock and to takeout below Lordville, where I was told access was possible, trout fishing was reasonably good and the chance of meeting fishing guides was minimal. I didn't have time to check out the launch and takeout sites on this section but I had them marked on my map. A big mistake.

We decided to make the downstream run first so we would be closer to our upstate homes on the second day. Ron Gugnacki, Gordon Potter, Bob McNitt and I met at a diner in Narrowsburg at 7 a.m. to discuss the trip over breakfast. Bob and I would fish from his Grumman aluminum canoe and Ron and Gordon would use my Mad River Explorer.

After unloading canoes and gear at the state launch, Bob and I drove downstream to park the takeout vehicle. When we returned, Ron and Gordon were already catching fish in the big pool at the launch site. We should have spent a half hour or so catching bass and perch from this "small lake" but we had a day of canoe-fishing ahead, so we paddled under the Narrowsburg bridge and into the river. A huge school of carp—big ones—crossed ahead of the canoe, seeking deeper water.

As I looked down the spring-green valley, sun glistening off the river, the sound of water rushing over rocks, the feel of the paddle and canoe in the current, it struck me—**I was actually canoe-fishing the Delaware River!** It was more spectacular than I imagined. The river was wide, the valley deep-sided and colored in every imaginable shade of green. Wildflowers bloomed along the shoreline. Overhead in a clear blue sky, hawks and turkey vultures soared. Later in the day we saw a bald eagle.

We drifted downstream, casting spinners, spoons and plugs, and caught a few bass and rockbass. When schools of shad passed under the canoes, we switched to shad darts. Ron had the first shad on, but lost it after a short battle. He yelled that it was just as strong as he remembered.

Ron and I had fished the Delaware years before by wading the waters near the mouth of Ten Mile River. We caught shad by casting into the current, letting the dart drift downstream, and then lifting the rod tip.

No jerking, just lifting, I told myself as Bob guided our canoe to some slick water below a large rock. *Cast the dart, let the line go slack, reel in to straighten the line and then lift the rod tip.* Two cranks, two lifts ... and wham ... the rod tip danced and the reel drag sang. I held on, keeping the line tight, while the fish crisscrossed in front of the canoe, jumping only once. We netted and released a 3-pound female American shad. My arms ached, it felt great.

We saw many more shad in the river, and even had a few on for a couple of minutes, but just couldn't hang on to them. We also caught more bass, some rockbass and long ear sunfish, but nothing fought like the shad.

We used the anchor quite a bit to hold above slick water and pools, not realizing that the rocks in this area were sawing away at our anchor line. When the anchor finally cut loose, we stopped for a stretch, a snack and to rig a substitute anchor. It was during this break that we discovered the source of the loud chirping we had heard along the river.

The chorus stopped when we pulled into shore, but by the time Bob had turned a hatchet-shaped rock into an anchor and we had filled our bellies with coffee, oreos and apples, the chirping resumed in earnest. Along the shoreline we watched some large toads fill their throats with air to call prospective mates. I had heard and seen small toads do this near ponds and lakes upstate, but never encountered this larger species in action.

We caught up to Ron and Gordon just upstream from a railroad bridge. They had seen schools of shad and some American eels and had caught some bass and hooked and lost a few shad.

Upstream from the bridge a long patch of slick water looked good, so Bob lowered the anchor just above it. Before the anchor touched bottom, the shad I mentioned at the beginning of this story was flying out of the water. Minutes later Bob was scaring the life out of me trying to take pictures of the fish and help me net it. He did both and we didn't even come close to tipping over, but fighting a leaping fish is enough excitement without someone walking around in an anchored canoe in moving water — not recommended unless you're prepared for a dunking.

Other than my personal scare, the only close call we had was negotiating what looked to be a short rapids or rock shelf across the river. The rule is to look for the downstream V because that's the safest path through obstructions. In this case the downstream V was the middle of an eel weir. Before we got hung up on what looked like a metal or plywood ramp, we veered off to the left, bumped the bottom a couple of times and reached safe water. I understand there are several other eel weirs along the river, but we saw only one on this stretch.

When we beached the canoes that afternoon, we were already making plans for a return trip the following year.

On the second day, after a much needed night's rest at Smith's Colonial Motel on Route 97, south of Hancock, we were looking forward to a big breakfast at the Circle E Diner. That breakfast was the beginning of a memorable day.

When the cook/waiter and presumed proprietor came to our table with four cups of coffee, we asked for a menu and if he had Eggbeaters. His answers: "No menu. Tell me what you want and I'll tell you if I got it" and "If you want Eggbeaters go to the hospital." After taking our orders which consisted of various combinations of eggs, meat and pancakes, he returned with a handful of silverware and dropped it in the middle of the table. In 10 minutes he was back with our orders, cooked perfectly.

I was told that the best place to launch was on the PA side at Buckingham, north of the Lordville bridge, but that a PA boat stamp costing $10 was required to launch there. That seemed kind of expensive for a single canoe launch, so I opted for the public access pulloff downriver. That access turned out to be a steep climb over rocks and through trees, so we took our chances and drove to Buckingham and launched the canoes without incident.

Back at Lordville we drove down the east side of the river to the state land where I was told we could park the takeout vehicle close to the river. Not quite. A half mile from the river some signs announced no motor vehicles were allowed, although there were tire tracks in the road. Time was a'waisting, so we followed the road to the railroad tracks, parked Bob's Jeep in the woods and returned to the launched canoes.

Gordon had taken the first fish from this "trout" water while we were gone. It was a walleye. Figures. This was not a normal day. It was almost 9 o'clock and cloudy when we finally got underway.   By 10 o'clock it was raining. Should have been a great day for fishing. We paddled through long stretches of flatwater, catching a smallmouth or rockbass now and then. When we reached riffles and runs, two or three fly fishermen were standing in the middle of them being coached by river guides.

Despite the disappointing fishing and occasional rain shower, our five-mile run was still an adventure. Although not as spectacular as downstream, the river was still beautiful with the spring greens of soft maple, birch, cherry and sycamore along the shore and hillsides.

We saw wood ducks, mallards and mergansers. Near the mouth of Equinunk Creek we found a flock of turkey vultures resting (perhaps nesting) in trees and on a rocky bluff overlooking the river. When Ron and Gordon tried to fish in a small bay, two mute swans chased them back to the river. The swans had a nest on a tiny island.

Downstream from the bluff, Ron caught the only trout of the entire trip, a 15-inch brown that hit a shad dart. Bob caught a pickerel, also on a shad dart, in the same area. We saw some shad in the river, but hooked only one.

Below Lordsville, just before the takeout, we watched a fly fisherman fight and land a nice rainbow in a long riffle, proof positive that this area holds some nice trout.

Bob's Jeep was still where we left it—no tickets, no notes on the windshield. We returned to the launch site to get my vehicle and left Ron and Gordon to carry the gear and canoes up the bank and over the railroad tracks. On the way I told Bob we should have launched at Hancock and taken out at Lordville. It would have been a longer trip but access is easy, legal and hassle-free.

On the way home we discussed our plans for next year. We decided to make the downstream run an annual event—bigger river, faster water, fewer fishermen, more fish and easy access. Perhaps we'll give the trout water another try—someday.

For information on this area write: Information, Upper Delaware Scenic and Recreation River, National Park Service, POB K, Narrowsburg, NY 12764. For information on fish and fishing write: NYS DEC Region 3, Fisheries, 21 South Putt Corners Rd., New Paltz, NY 12561-1696 and PA Fish and Boat Commission, NE Region, POB 88, Sweet Valley, PA 18656. For information on Special Delaware River fishing regulations refer to the New York Fishing Regulations Guide you get when you buy your license.

EAST BRANCH CROTON RIVER

There I was canoe-fishing a stream not much wider than the canoe with a world-class angler. He had caught salmon and trout in Alaska and Canada, permit on the Florida Flats; he had fished countless rivers and lakes in the United States and in other countries. He was a former editor of "Field & Stream" magazine and was at that moment president of the Outdoor Writers Association of America. How much fun could this be for him? It didn't take long to find out.

Glenn Sapir lives on the east side of the Hudson River near Peekskill. When I asked him to point me in the direction of a stream to canoe-fish in his area, he suggested the headwaters of the East Branch of the Croton River in northeastern Putnam County.

"You'll like it Paul. Flows through the "Great Swamp" where there is plenty of wildlife. There are some panfish in the river and the last time I was there we saw a number of carp. I'll be happy to go with you if we can work it out."

A subsequent discussion with a DEC fisheries biologist revealed that the stretch of the East Branch below the swamp and closer to East Branch Reservoir was good trout water. We couldn't cover the entire run in one day, so we stuck to our original plans to canoe-fish Great Swamp.

We wanted to make a spring run when both wildlife and carp are most active, but just couldn't get together until early fall. After parking Glenn's car at the takeout bridge on Route 22 just north of Route 164, we drove the three miles back to launch the canoe at the bridge on Route 311 near Aikins Corners. It was 1 p.m.

We didn't have any idea what kind of fish would be in the river at this time of year, so we rigged our fishing rods with spinners and plastic jigs and brought along some carp bait. Just below the bridge was a large pool ringed with weeds and fallen trees. Glenn's white Rooster Tail produced an immediate follow. A brightly-colored brook trout trailed the spinner to the boat and disappeared in a swirl.

"Did you see the color of that fish?", Glenn asked, obviously excited.

Trout? I thought all the trout were miles downstream. The river was blocked by a downed tree at the far end of the pool. A cast in this area produced a 9-inch brown trout. What was going on here? This was swamp water, panfish and carp habitat.

Glenn held up his fish before releasing it so I could take some pictures. After we carried the canoe around the fallen tree and continued downriver, Glenn saw a fish rise in a long pool just ahead of the canoe. Under overhanging branches, he flipped his spinner at the rings left by the rise. Nothing. Another cast a few feet downstream was gobbled up by another brown trout, a 10 incher this time.

The smile on Glenn's face was worth the long drive from my home upstate. He was really enjoying catching pan-size trout from this tiny stream. As we paddled and pushed the canoe through brush and fallen trees from one pool to another, Glenn suggested that we switch positions so I could cast more often. I declined. He was having too much fun.

The first mile or so was littered with fallen trees, so we had to paddle, push, and sometimes carry the canoe downstream. When we reached a graded parking area where we saw some Fish & Wildlife Cooperator Area signs, the stream appeared wider and most of the blowdowns had been cut back to allow easy canoeing. For a time we enjoyed drifting along in the canoe, casting now and then to good looking water or an occasional rise. We soon realized that while the canoeing was easier catching fish was not. Except for a few follows we couldn't raise another fish. Oh well, downstream we were sure to find some carp, maybe even some pickerel and rock bass. Time to look around and get to know the river.

I had never canoe-fished such a stream. While the surrounding land seemed extremely flat, like in most swamps, the current was significant in all but the deepest pools and areas dammed by fallen trees. This was painfully evident when I tried to stop the canoe by grabbing a shoreline tree or branch. Almost yanked my arm out of the socket a couple of times.

The stream bed was not mud as I expected, it was sand. In areas where the sun reached the water through shoreline trees and brush, we could see shiny flecks on the bottom. Gold? More likely pyrite. Glenn jokingly suggested a return trip with his Montana gold pan.

In some areas a coarse grass grew on the stream bottom, providing fish cover and creating interesting formations. One of these formations looked like a porcupine, another like an exotic under-sea plant.

Streamside vegetation was different than any other stream I had canoe-fished in the state. There were very few cattails, swamp grasses or alders. Tall slender plants, topped with clusters of leaves dominated the vegetation in shallow water. Taller brush, some with individual (not clustered) red berries, grew just out of the water. Widely spaced trees gave the woods on both sides of the river a park-like appearance. Many of these trees were maples, most I didn't recognize. Even some of the maples were different than I had seen before. The leaves were broader and had less points than either the silver or sugar maples I was most familiar with.

Wildlife? Where was all the wildlife? Apparently deer inhabited the swamp because we saw a few tree stands in one area. We had also seen a number of wood duck houses. There were plenty of small bays and backed up pools along the river ideal for mallards, blacks and woodies. We saw one black duck, a couple of doves, a kingfisher, a woodpecker, some song birds and a turtle. That was it. Early fall was not the time to see wildlife in Great Swamp.

It was also not the time to see carp either. It would have been fun to latch onto a big carp in such a small stream, but we didn't see even one of these much maligned bruisers. No rock bass or pickerel either.

We saw a few rises and had a couple of hits, but didn't connect with a single fish for the rest of the trip.

When we heard the traffic on Route 22 it was 5:30. A half hour later we were loading the canoe on Glenn's car. The three miles traveled by car was a good six miles by canoe. It had been an interesting and enjoyable outing. Nothing like I expected and quite different from what Glenn had experienced on previous trips.

Upon reflection some of the reasons the East Branch of the Croton River of spring and the East Branch of fall are so different become less mysterious. The warming waters of spring and the desire to spawn attract carp from the lower reservoir. Cooling waters and the spawning cycles of browns and brookies bring them upstream to the Great Swamp in the fall. (Trout season closes on September 30th.)

Waterfowl are most active during the spring when they gather for nesting and raising young. Most of the ducks raised on this tiny stream move to bigger waters later in the year. We didn't see deer or the other wildlife that were surely there because we were making so much noise talking or paddling and pushing the canoe.

The rest remains a mystery to me.

OTHER SOUTHERN
RIVERS AND STREAMS
TO CANOE-FISH

WAPPINGER CREEK
PECONIC RIVER (LONG ISLAND)

The Delaware River is spectacular anytime of year, but when American shad are spawning in the river, canoe-fishing can be very exciting—especially when your partner is standing up in the canoe taking pictures.

This midstream rock on Rondout Creek offered an ideal place for Ron Gugnacki to position the canoe out of the current to fish a short run and a deep pool for walleye and rockbass.

After a day of catching smallmouth bass and some walleyes from the Tioga & Chemung Rivers, Mike Warren hooked this 12-pound Tiger Muskie when we anchored the canoe just upstream from the Route 17 Bridge in Corning.

When we fished Oswayo Creek and the Allegheny River in mid September we discovered the smallmouths had moved out of the creek and into the deeper runs of the river. We took a few big bass, like this one held by Tom Murray, on gold spinners and plugs.

CHAPTER 12

WESTERN RIVERS AND STREAMS

Map indicates general location of rivers and streams discussed and otherwise noted in this chapter

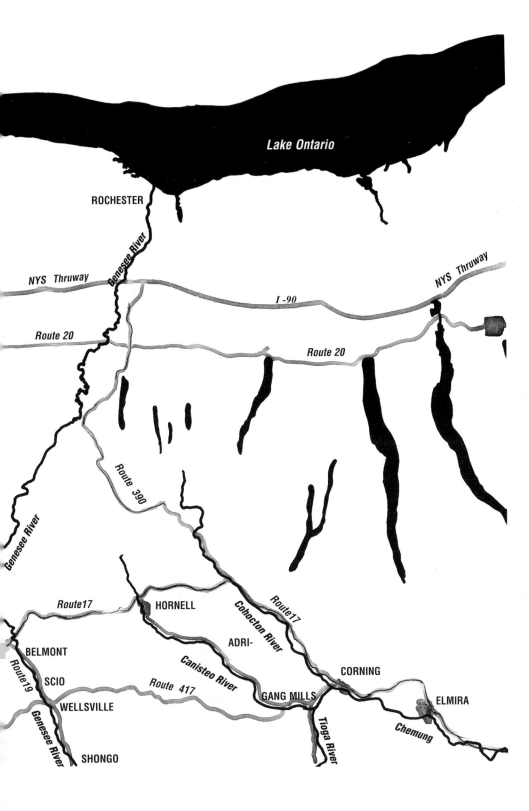

Our spring run down the Upper Genesee was the ideal time to catch trout and see a variety of wildlife. Tom Murray took a 13 and a 15-inch brown from one hole on a C.P. Swing.

John Pitarresi fishes the Canisteo River right after a half-day of thunder-storms. Normally productive bass and walleye havens wouldn't give up a single fish when the river was high and dirty.

UPPER GENESEE RIVER

"Show me a brown trout and I'll show you this Phoebe can catch fish.", I quipped as Tom Murray landed his sixth rainbow trout on a C.P. Swing. I considered giving up on the gold spoon, but Dutch stubbornness wouldn't let me, not this early in the game anyway.

As we approached a deep run that was partially shaded, Tom dropped his gold spinner in the middle of it. The spinner flashed as it emerged from darkness into sunlight. Three fish were following it, one was a big brown trout. The big brown followed the lure to midstream, turned tail and disappeared into the shade.

My Phoebe hit the dark water a few seconds later, pulsed at the end of my ultralight spinning rod for a few seconds more, then stopped. I set the hook, loosened the drag on my reel and enjoyed the feel of a strong fish at the end of light line. I didn't have to say it, but I did anyway. "Like I said, show me a brown."

My moment of glory was short lived and never returned for the two days Tom and I canoe-fished the Upper Genesee River near Wellsville in late May. Tom and his gold spinners outfished me and all my lures more often than I care to tell.

Tom Murray works for the New York State Department of Environmental Conservation as a Principal Fisheries Technician out of the Olean office, so he knows the Upper Genesee River well and fishes it often. Although he has always waded this stream and prefers fly fishing, he agreed to join me in a canoe, spinfishing for early season trout.

Tom had little canoeing experience and I had never been on the Upper Genesee before so this was an adventure for both of us. To get used to the canoe and each other, Tom selected a short stretch of the river from Wellsville to Scio, along Route 19. We launched my Sportspal at the bridge off Route 417, not far from the McDonalds where we met for coffee.

I couldn't tell if Tom was excited about fishing the river or apprehensive about canoeing it, so I made a point of explaining that the Sportspal is more like a barge than a canoe, and that it was almost impossible to tip over. I failed to mention that low overhanging branches could sweep us out of the canoe, but he learned that the second day.

The stretch we fished below Wellsville consists of long riffs, a few short rapids and some deep runs and pools. Trees border much of the river, providing some shade even in the middle of the day.

Tom noted that this area is more "civilized" than the upstream area we would run the following day. As if to emphasize that point we passed over several golf balls that had escaped from a nearby country club.

This section of the stream is well-stocked with both rainbow and brown trout, and Tom noted that later in the year smallmouth bass become very active, especially in the deep runs and pools. We didn't catch a single bass, but the trout were very cooperative ... for Tom anyway. He started catching fish almost as soon as we launched the canoe, and continued to catch all the fish until he found me that big brown.

His entire arsenal for trout was an assortment of C. P. Swing spinners. The rainbows ate them up. I stuck with my Phoebe spoon for a half hour or so after I caught the big brown, but switched to a Mepps and a Panther Martin spinners to get in on the action.

Despite nearby civilization, wildlife was abundant all along the river. Both mallards and mergansers—mostly males—jumped off the river as we approached, flew downstream or circled overhead. A couple of great blue herons kept us company and crows announced our arrival at almost every bend in the river. A woodchuck didn't hear or ignored their warning, because it didn't miss a beat as it dug full speed into the river bank as we canoed just a few feet away.

When we pulled out at Scio, I was a fan of the Upper Genesee River and Tom was getting hooked on fishing from a canoe. Despite the many hours he had worked on this stream and the many years he had fished it, we canoed through areas he had never seen before.

The following day we met at the Deli on South Main St. in Wellsville at 8 a.m. It was 30 degrees outside so we didn't hurry our coffee and bagels. Tom explained that we would put in not far from the Pennsylvania border and canoe through some of the most remote sections of the river. We could expect to catch browns, rainbows and perhaps a big brook trout. Each year a few of the breeder brookies that PA stocks upstream move into the area and are caught by local anglers. It doesn't take long for the word to spread that a 2–3 pound brook trout was taken from the Genesee River.

Actually the river in this area is more like a brook, meandering through hardwoods and over riffles and mini rapids from one small

pool to the next, with a few deep runs mixed in here and there. In
many areas there was barely enough water to float the canoe. We
had to walk it through some short stretches and carry around fallen
trees. This was not easy canoeing, but well worth every effort,
every obstacle.

Not 50 yards from where we put in, two deer stood midstream,
the sun shining off their spring coats. They were surprised but not
startled. Tails down they walked into the woods.

For the first part of the trip the trout were lockjawed, but
wildlife was so abundant and active I hardly noticed. Again mallards and mergansers seemed to be waiting at every bend in the
river. Kingfishers scolded from time to time, and flycatchers and
waxwings picked insects from the air above the water. A goose with
goslings disappeared into the high grass as we approached, and
Tom saw two more deer disappear into the woods.

We became so enthralled with seeing wildlife, we didn't notice
the low overhanging branches of a streamside maple as the canoe
entered a long, fast riffle. The branches almost "broomed" us out of
the canoe. Fortunately the water was shallow and we were wearing
hip boots, so I stepped out of the canoe and slowed it down while
Tom pushed, pulled and bullied our way through.

Much of this stretch of the Genesee River is designated "No
Kill" for trout. For the first couple of hours it was a "No Catch" area
for us. Then Tom got serious. While I took pictures and walked the
canoe through shallow water, Tom worked the holes—big and
small—with his gold spinners and started catching fish. He took
two nice browns—13 and 15 inches—from a hole that was partially filled with the giant roots of a long-dead tree. He hooked several more trout, and even let me latch on to a couple before we took
out at the bridge at York's Corners.

We met a number of stream fishermen along the way, most of
them had caught fish. Only two anglers had hiked in to fish out-of-
the-way holes and runs; most were fishing close to bridges. We
didn't see another canoe on the river, and from what information I
could gather, almost no one canoe-fishes the Upper Genesee.

As is the case with many streams in New York State, most of
this river is not fished, because it's so difficult to reach on foot.
However, under the right conditions these seldom-fished areas can
be reached with a canoe. On the Upper Genesee, especially the

stretch from the PA border to York's Corners, the right conditions for canoeing and catching fish are usually in May and early June. April water is a bit cold and high for consistent trout catching in most areas, and canoeing this stretch during periods of high water could be very dangerous with all the fallen trees, low overhanging branches and log-filled sharp turns. If you do give this area a try during high water, be sure to wear a life vest or jacket.

There are fewer obstacles and more water in the stretch from Wellsville to Scio, so it is much safer during high water and can be canoe-fished into the summer months. There is also some canoe-able water between York's Corners and Wellsville, but on the lower reaches of this stretch there are some low dams and dikes that require carries and care to negotiate.

The fun part of preparing this book is meeting new people, canoeing a variety of waters, seeing flora and fauna, and catching fish where almost no one casts a line. Canoe-fishing with Tom Murray on the Upper Genesee River was more fun than anyone really deserves.

In addition to the two sections we covered there is plenty of canoe-fishing water below Scio. For more information on the Upper Genesee River write to: NYS DEC, CFB, Region 9, Fisheries, 128 South St., Olean, NY 14760. For information on accommodations and attractions write to Cattaraugus-Allegany Tourist Bureau, 303 Court St., Little Valley, NY 14755.

CANISTEO RIVER

I had read John Pitarresi's outdoor column in the Utica paper for years, so I knew he was from the Niagara Falls area and often returned there to fish; he hunted deer with his family in Steuben County, and he loved fishing the streams in central and upstate New York. When I asked him to suggest a stream we could canoe-fish together, I was surprised when he chose a stream near his family's hunting camp.

The Canisteo River is born in the northwest corner of Steuben County, flows south through Hornell, swings to the southeast near the village of Canisteo and crosses the county diagonally until it enters the Tioga River near Corning. For much of its length it flows through steepsided valleys of shale and shaly sandstone, covered in most areas by glacial soils. Hardwoods grow on the hillsides and narrow farmfields fill the valley floor. This corridor of woods, fields and water has long been recognized as a good place to hunt whitetail deer and turkey. And, thanks to New York's "pure waters" laws it has also become a good place to fish.

Back in the 1960's John's grandfather bought a farmhouse and some land in this area to use as a hunting camp. Since then sons, grandsons, uncles and nephews have hunted the family "farm" for deer and turkey. We used this camp as our base of operations for canoe-fishing the Canisteo. Buck racks, turkey fans, beards and spurs, plus a pile of photographs attested to many successful hunts over the years. Among the photos was one of John's grandfather, at 91, with the last buck he had taken.

John's cousin, Will Tompkins from Niagara Falls was working around camp when we arrived at midday. He volunteered to help us get set up for an afternoon of canoe-fishing by dropping us off at the launch site at the bridge in Carson after we put our takeout vehicle at Catatunk Bridge in Adrian. While we canoe-fished this stretch of the river, Will planned to fish a couple of productive holes near camp.

The river didn't look good. Morning and midday thunder showers had raised the water level a good two feet and colored it chocolate brown. Definitely not the kind of conditions we preferred to fish for walleyes and bass, but we had planned this mid-June trip for months and couldn't make it any other time. We waited until 3:30 to launch the canoe.

As we cast spinners, plugs and jigs to the many runs, pools and downed trees, John explained why he wanted to canoe-fish the Canisteo. He and his cousins had often fished the river from shore or by wading in the area near their camp, and at times did very well on smallmouths and walleye. Except for the areas near bridges, there was very little fishing pressure, so fishing from a canoe and wading hard to reach stretches should be very productive.

A great blue heron preceded us downstream, lifting from the water each time we came into view. Mergansers were also fishing the river. I wondered if the high, dirty water was denying them dinner too. Although John managed to jig up some fallfish from a couple of deep runs, we didn't connect with a single bass or walleye.

The Canisteo in this area winds through farmlands, close to hardwood hills and past shale cliffs. Box elder, hemlock and a few pines shade river runs and pools. Wildflowers grow in profusion in many areas. Flocks colored the shoreline while we were there and filled the air with a natural perfume.

John had pointed out a number of runs where deer had crossed the river between wooded hills and farmlands, so we were on the lookout for deer. Near the end of our trip, a young doe, leaped off a high bank and bounded across the river, sun shining off splashing water. That sight made up for the poor fishing.

Although we fished some areas hard and long, the high fast water carried us along at a pretty good clip, so we were off the river by 6 o'clock. Back at camp we learned that Will hadn't caught a single fish from the "best holes on the river".

It rained again during the night, so we didn't hurry back to the river the next morning. We drove to Hornell to have breakfast and see Will on his way home before returning to the river to launch the canoe where we took out the night before. (We had parked the take-out vehicle at Brown's Crossing.)

The hardwoods on each side of the valley held a heavy mist that looked like smoke. Overhead a path of clear blue sky grew ever wider until by 10 a.m. the sun was shining on the river. Unfortunately, the river raged with brown water that was higher than the day before. Oh well, we were committed.

I'm not an expert canoeist, that's why I don't canoe-fish during the spring runoff and stay away from expert class waters, preferring easywater whenever possible. But the Canisteo that morning was running at near springtime conditions, so I made every effort to avoid downed trees and piles of logs, especially at the outside bends in the river. During high water such places can be very dangerous because the water moves so fast and in so many directions it's difficult to control a canoe.

Because John had had little canoeing experience, I couldn't rely on him to get us out of trouble like I often do with more experienced partners. Part of our adventure that morning was getting through some waters that wanted to take us into trees and logs. We managed to avoid all those obstacles but one. In anticipation of such a situation, I had told John that sometimes the best thing to do to avoid trouble is to get out of the canoe. I have used the "when in doubt, jump out" tactic a number of times over the years with great success.

We had passed through a short riff and into a long pool that just had to hold fish. We worked the pool with spinners all the way to the tail end. I could see the fast water at the end of the pool, but didn't see the log stuck in the middle of it. By the time I had paddle in hand, the river had already decided that we needed to be pushed up against that log, a very dangerous situation. While we were still in shallow water, I yelled to John to get out of the canoe. He did, I did, and we walked the canoe to shore without a problem. Something to be said for jumping ship.

Fortunately, the only witnesses to our lack of canoeing skills were some mallards, mergansers, muskrats, a great blue heron and a couple of turkey vultures.

Around noon, near the end of the run, the water cleared up slightly, and we started to catch fish. Nothing spectacular, but enough to get an idea how good the fishing would be under better conditions. A gold spinner produced smallmouth bass up to 13 inches and an 18-inch walleye, plus a couple of rock bass and fall-fish. We found most of these fish near the deep run and rocks along side the railroad tracks above Brown's Crossing. I learned later that a good friend and fellow canoe-fisherman, Mike Warren had taken a 5-pound walleye from this same water.

Well, John didn't get to show me how good the fishing was on his river, but sometimes you have to fish when you can, not when conditions are ideal. We did see a beautiful valley and plenty of wildlife. We had a few thrills and caught a few fish. I got to know John better, got to meet Will and visit the "farm". All in all, a very good weekend.

TIOGA-CHEMUNG RIVERS

"I canoe-fished the Chemung from Corning east and took plenty of smallmouth bass. Caught a four-pounder right in Corning. Local anglers take some big walleyes and tiger muskies every year.

I've also fished a few spots on the Tioga from shore and always caught bass. So, if we start on the Tioga and take out on the Chemung we should catch bass, some walleyes and maybe even a tiger—and you'll have canoe-fished two streams in our area." Mike Warren explained over the phone as we finalized plans for a late June outing.

Mike writes outdoor articles for the Hornell newspaper and is a Regional Editor for the *NEW YORK SPORTSMAN* magazine. I've read his articles for a number of years, so I know he does a lot more than just write about the outdoors; he fishes and hunts extensively in western New York. I guessed he would know a stream or two where we could canoe-fish easywater. I guessed right.

We unloaded my Sportspal in the parking lot at the Old Grove Diner upstream from Gang Mills on the road that runs along the river off Route 417. The clay bank to the river was steep and slippery, so we took our time getting canoe and gear to the water. It was a perfect day: about 60 degrees, a few clouds, sun just coming up and almost no wind.

Neither of us had ever canoe-fished the Tioga and it was my canoe, so as tradition dictates I offered Mike the bow seat. I didn't have to offer twice. Mike knew that while the stern paddler controls the canoe and works the anchor, the guy in the front seat can keep on fishing. That arrangement would prove very fortunate for Mike before the trip ended.

I rigged my ultralight with a gold Blue Fox spinner and another spinning rod with a small floating Rapala. Mike selected a battered and beaten Rebel Wee Crawfish for his light spinning rod. His other rod—a heavy-duty model loaded with 10-pound Magna Thin line— seemed out of place in a canoe. When I asked what he expected to catch with "that thing," he reminded me that there were some big fish in the river.

We didn't find any of those big fish at the first bridge we came to, but a hungry smallmouth smacked Mike's crayfish imitation and held on until he lifted it into the canoe. Mike repeated that catch in a hole below a large island. Nothing was interested in my Rapala, so I switched to a spanking new Wee Crawfish. Mike caught another bass. I caught nothing although we seemed to be fishing in the same kind of water. When we compared lures, Mike noted that his old lure didn't have a rattle in it, but my new lure did. He had some of the newer Crawfish but always caught more fish on the older models. He certainly proved it to my satisfaction by catching four bass to my one all day long.

I did have some luck with the heavy gold spinner. Downstream from another island the Tioga formed a long relatively deep run. I cast my spinner into the area where the currents from both sides of the island merged, and then let it drift into the run. As soon as I started to retrieve my offering, a walleye ate it. After releasing the fish, I paddled to shore so we could wade. A cast just downstream from where I had caught the walleye from the canoe produced a sudden stop and then a slow steady drive upstream. With the ultra-light held high and bent to the water, I tried to turn the fish. Before I could yell to Mike that I had one of those big fish on, it was gone.

Around mid morning only a few clouds remained in the sky and the sun penetrated all but the east side of the river where maples and willows provided a corridor of shade. We caught smallmouths in water that was less than a foot deep all along that shrinking corridor.

Our next stop was at a railroad bridge where we beached the canoe to eat lunch, fish the bridge abutments and downstream pools, and watch a train move back and forth across the river. The engineer waved just before we passed under the bridge. While we ate and fished, he moved cars in and out of what appeared to be a small switch yard. Mike caught a few smallmouths near the abutments and I took pictures.

When we reached the point where the Cohocton enters the Tioga there was no significant change in the river other than it turned direction from north to east. The valley was just as broad, the river was just as wide and the water level looked the same. Yet the name of the river changed from Tioga to Chemung. Perhaps the Tioga was named where it starts in Pennsylvania and the Chemung was named further downstream on the New York side of the border —no doubt long before there was a border. In any case I couldn't in good conscience consider this two canoe-fishing streams, hence the title Tioga - Chemung Rivers.

There are some good pools in this area of the Chemung. We caught bass from the pools and from the waters near some large rocks that line the shore. As the Route 17 bridge in Corning came into view, Mike noted we were approaching one of the hottest spots on the river for big walleyes and tiger muskies. With that announcement he attached a silver-bladed, black-skirted spinner bait trailed by a chartreuse curlytail, to his heavy-duty spinning rod.

Most of the really big fish are taken by shoreline anglers casting big minnow imitations or spinner baits, so we headed for the pier near the center of the bridge that would be most difficult to fish from shore. While I lowered the anchor upstream from the bridge, Mike made his first cast above the pier. As the anchor grabbed bottom and the canoe swung into position, Mike made his second cast. It dropped the spinner bait right next to the pier ..... and into the mouth of a big fish. Mike's "stick" bent to the fish and gave up line in long gasps.

Before I realized what I was doing, the anchor line was coming in hand over hand and the canoe was following the big fish downstream. Mike's fishing skills and choice of tackle brought the big fish to the surface, but because we didn't have a net he was certain he would never land it. I paddled the canoe around the bridge piers, out of the current and into shallow water. When the sun reflected off a three-foot, iridescent-blue, striped tiger muskie, we held our breaths and stepped out of the canoe. Mike kept the rod tip high while I wrapped the fingers of one hand around the tail and slid the other hand up to the fish's belly.

We had every intention of releasing Mike's trophy, but the fight, a bloody cut from the hook and the time we took to take photographs had apparently taken their toll, because all our efforts to revive and release that tiger proved futile. It wasn't wasted, however, because Mike and his family ate it and had it mounted. It weighed 12 pounds and measured an even 36 inches.

With the tiger and a half dozen fat bass in tow, we drifted through Corning, casting halfheartedly to shoreline rocks. There are no buildings near the river on the Chemung in this area. A history of massive flooding had long ago relegated the shoreline to rows of willow trees and grassy slopes that are well maintained. As we passed under a mid-town bridge and past water outlets, Mike pointed out areas where he had caught some big smallmouths while fishing from shore. When we reached our takeout vehicle near the north end of Conhocton St., at the east end of town it was 2:30 p.m.

After stopping to ice Mike's fish, we returned to the Old Grove Diner to pick up our launch vehicle and for a late lunch. Over soup and sandwiches we recounted the day. I was surprised at how little wildlife we saw. Except for a great blue heron, a couple of mergansers, a wood duck and a muskrat, we were the only critters traveling the river all day long. I was elated at the number of fish we encountered. Mike was ecstatic about his first-ever tiger muskie.

Mike noted that while the city of Corning promotes the Glass Center and the downtown shopping areas in brochures and advertisements, they never mention how good the fishing is in the river. Perhaps that's just as well. I like the idea of canoe-fishermen and their families spending a day or so in Corning seeing the attractions and then enjoying the river all by themselves.

OSWAYO CREEK

I like the sound of "Oswayo". "A-sway-o" ... sounds peaceful, relaxing, almost mystical. It's an Indian name of course, or at least the English interpretation of an Indian name. No one seems to know for sure what it means, so I suppose "magic waters" will do, or how about "small stream with big fish". That was our experience anyway when we canoe-fished this tributary of the Allegheny River in western New York in mid September.

Tom Murray and I launched the canoe at the bridge at Ceres, right on the New York - Pennsylvania border. It was 50 degrees and a thick fog enveloped the creek. As we drifted downstream, drooping willows and silver maples loomed out of the mist. We could hear the sound of riffles ahead, but all we could see was a wall of white. The forecast called for a sunny day, so the fog wouldn't last long.

Neither of us had ever canoe-fished the Oswayo, but Tom is a Principal Fisheries Technician for DEC at the Olean office, so he knew that we could expect to catch smallmouth bass and maybe even a muskie in the many pools and runs we would encounter throughout the day. The Oswayo is also home to some big carp, so we could fish for them if nothing else was interested in our offerings.

While the six-mile stretch we decided to canoe-fish from Ceres to Toll Gate Corner on Route 417 starts and ends in New York, the first couple of miles are in Pennsylvania. There is no reciprocal fishing license agreement for this area, so both PA and New York licenses are required to legally fish the entire run.

The Oswayo looked like a trout stream to me, with long riffles and runs, swirling pools, undercut banks, lots of logs and rocks and plenty of shade, but Tom assured me that there were no trout in this area of the creek. As if to prove the point he rigged his spinning rod with a no-name, bright gold, floating minnow imitation that had taken more than its share of smallmouths and northerns. I rigged one ultralight with a floating perch Rapala, the other with a gold Panther Martin.

Tom flipped his lure to a small but deep pool, let it sit for a couple seconds and then started the retrieve. A white-sided torpedo swirled at the lure and missed ... disappeared ... and then returned to engulf the lure. After a brief battle Tom landed and released a 20-inch muskie. Nice start.

As the sun dissipated the fog, we could see upstream and down. In addition to the willows and maples, oak, birch and beech leaned over the water, providing a canopy of leaves in some areas. All was green except for a few maples that had just started turning red. Under this canopy wisps of moisture rose from the river like ghostly stalagmites.

A pair of mergansers ran off the water and flew downstream.

The canoe drifted slowly along the left bank, but the creek ran with a rush on the right bank, allowing us to cast into what looked like smallmouth bass water. A gouge in the creek bank the size of a compact car formed a deep hole right under an overhanging maple. There just had to be a bass (or in my stubborn mind a brown trout) waiting for an easy meal. The first cast produced nothing. Second cast ... nothing. Third ... still nothing.

One more cast before I was out of range. The perch Rapala was almost back to the boat when a fish flashed by and disappeared. Before I finished the sentence, "A big fish made a pass at my lure", it came back, smacked the Rapala and held on. For five minutes I fought a two-foot plus, deep-sided muskellunge on my ultralight. When I finally had it next to the boat, it dove for the bottom and was gone.

We heard the crows before we saw them. Sounded like a large flock and they were mad, very mad. Tom reasoned their wrath was directed at a hawk. I noted that every time I had heard a similar raucous the crows had treed an owl. When the flock of some 25 noisy crows came into view, they were circling a large tree but moved off when they saw us drifting down the creek. As we approached the center of their attention, a large owl flew across the river ... followed by a big red-tailed hawk. When we were right under that tree, a smaller hawk took flight. Certainly explained why the crows were so angry.

Tom took another muskie from a hole under a tree. It fought well for a few minutes and then threw the lure. It struck me that we were fishing in a relatively small stream that was just loaded with ideal trout and bass cover, but all we could "catch" was 2–3 foot muskellunge on ultralight tackle. Tough to take.

When the sun warmed the creek, we saw carp everywhere. They passed under, around and ahead of the canoe. In one area we "herded" a dozen big carp down the creek for several minutes. Huge suckers swam under the canoe in shallow pools and runs, sometimes right alongside the carp.

There were no homes along this stretch of the Oswayo. The only signs of life were the birds we encountered, and the tracks of whitetail deer, beaver and raccoon in the mud at water's edge. The creek was quite clean and except for some tires lying on the bottom, it seemed far from civilization.

We stopped to stretch our legs and fish some riffles and runs near some old wooden pilings. My gold spinner enticed a couple of small bass from the fast water below a long riffle.

I yelled to Tom, "Look at that. Have you ever seen anything so beautiful?" The sun had reached the exact angle where its rays passed through overhanging trees and reflected off the long upstream riffle. The rippling water looked like a river of diamonds flowing through a tunnel of trees. Magic!

We returned to the canoe and drifted towards some ancient bridge abutments. Tom cast his plug into a small bay just upstream from the abandoned crossing ... and it happened again. A long fish made a pass at the lure, disappeared and returned to take the bait. When Tom lifted the fish into the boat I was surprised to see it was a northern pike. It measured 26 inches. As we passed by the bridge abutments, Tom cast his deadly lure into the deep water next to the center pier. The lure stopped when an even bigger pike ate it. It was 28 inches long.

Northern pike? I thought this was muskie water. Tom explained that the Allegheny River and its tributaries were traditionally home to muskellunge, but after northern pike were stocked in the Kinzua Reservoir by Federal fisheries people, they moved upstream into the river and creeks. They're now competing with muskies for food and cover.

Our next stop was at a steel bridge. The pools near the bridge looked good, but we didn't raise a single fish. Back to the canoe and on to more productive water. As we passed under some "singing" power lines and rounded a bend in the creek, a large flock of mergansers resting on a gravel bar flew downstream towards our take-out point at the Route 305 bridge.

For the last half mile we didn't catch anymore fish, and we never did find any respectable smallmouths. Tom noted that they had apparently moved out of the creek for their fall and winter stay in the deeper waters of the Allegheny. Perhaps we would find them the next day when we canoe-fished the river.

Heh, I'll trade smallmouths for muskie and northern pike any day of the week. When you add the wildlife ... and the magic ... well, it doesn't get any better than the Oswayo in September. Not in my book anyway.

ALLEGHENY RIVER

The Allegheny flows north into southwestern New York from Pennsylvania, sweeps west through Cattaraugus County and the communities of Olean and Salamanca, and returns south to PA through the Kinzua Reservoir. It's big water, especially during the spring runoff when the river is contained by a series of dikes that protect nearby communities. Most stretches of the river are too slow moving for my kind of canoe-fishing, so I asked DEC Principal Fisheries Technician, Tom Murray to select a section where there is plenty of current and plenty of fish.

Tom has spent most of his adult life working with fish. He nets fish, shocks fish, tags fish, counts fish, stocks fish and studies fish for a living. Over the years I've known many fisheries professionals who were so involved in working with fish, they didn't enjoy playing with fish. It didn't take long for me to discover that Tom has no such problem. He loves to fish.

We first met when we canoe-fished the Upper Genesee River. After that two-day adventure, I asked him to inquire about some other western New York streams that were suitable for easywater canoe-fishing. The following year he suggested Oswayo Creek for a full day and a section of the Allegheny River for a half-day outing. We planned to get together in early summer, but heavy rains made both streams too high and dirty for safe canoeing and good fishing. We had to wait until September.

Over breakfast at the Spring Hill Restaurant on Route 417 near Portville, we discussed the success of the previous day on the Oswayo and our hopes for finding fish on the Allegheny. We expected to find some good smallmouth in the deeper river waters and might even latch onto a good muskie. Earlier in the year Tom was on the river with a "shock boat" and brought up some 30-inch plus fish.

After dropping our takeout vehicle at the bridge at Steam Valley Road north of Portville, we drove south to launch the canoe at the bridge at Mill Grove, off Route 305 on West River Road. By the time we pushed through some fallen trees into the river it was 9 a.m. and the morning fog had all but dissipated.

The sun was shining, the sky was blue and a slight breeze rustled through grass and leaves. Grey squirrels dropped acorns from streamside oaks. Three mergansers and a great blue heron flew downstream ahead of us. It was a beautiful day.

Wooden pilings poked up through the river, creating a maze of easily negotiated obstructions. Tom explained that the pilings were the remains of dams and chutes that once controlled the flow of logs down the river. They also looked like ideal fish havens, so we cast spinners and plugs at them. No takers.

I caught the first fish, a smallmouth that ate a spinner in midstream. A small school of bass followed the fish to the boat, but we didn't linger in that area—too lazy to drop the anchor. We did linger at the mouth of Oswayo Creek where we beached the canoe and fished up the creek and where creek and river waters merge. Except for one small bass, no fish. I took a few pictures and we returned to the canoe.

Taking a clue from the school of bass we saw earlier, we concentrated on the deeper mid-river runs where there were no visible obstructions. Tom worked a large plug that looked like a gold minnow that was in big trouble. I reeled and jerked a gold Blue Fox spinner that weighed just enough to swim off the bottom in moving water. We both caught fish.

Tom's first was a two-foot northern pike that took the plug on the first pass. Mine was a 2-pound smallmouth that was holding in deep water several yards from a row of wooden pilings. Tom took a twin to my fish. Had we anchored and thoroughly fished this area, there was no doubt we could have caught a couple of limits of bass, but there was more river to cover.

As we moved into shallow water, huge carp swam ahead or cut cross stream. Tom saw a muskie rocket away from the canoe, reminding him of the big muskies he had seen during his tour on the shock boat. He noted that the pool at the takeout bridge was home to a couple of big muskies. Maybe, just maybe we'd get lucky.

Along the way an osprey lifted off a huge oak and soared downstream looking for an easy meal. A green heron left a streamside perch and disappeared in the trees, and a flock of mergansers beat the water with their wings before disappearing downriver.

On this lower stretch of the Allegheny flood control dikes parallel the river well back from the water's edge. It seemed we were on a river within a river. Doesn't look natural or pretty, but the people who live nearby don't complain, especially when the river rises to flood levels.

We caught a few more bass, always in deep runs, before reaching the bridge where Tom knew that at least a couple of big muskies looked for easy meals. We spent a half-hour trying to convince them that wooden minnows were easy meals, but they weren't interested. Oh well, our bass tackle was too light to land them anyway.

We had found where the bass were holding, so it was tempting to continue downstream, but I had a long drive home, so we called it a day around noon. This stretch of the Allegheny River has real possibilities, especially when smallmouth bass concentrate here in the fall. And, there is always the chance that a big muskie will decide to eat anything that swims.

For more information about the Allegheny River write: NYS DEC, Region 9, 128 South St., Olean, NY 14760. For more information about this area write: Cattaraugus-Allegany Tourist Bureau, 303 Court St., Little Valley, NY 14755.

OTHER WESTERN RIVERS AND STREAMS TO CANOE-FISH

COHOCTON RIVER
OAK ORCHARD CREEK
TONAWANDA CREEK

APPENDIX ONE

"RIGHTS OF PASSAGE"

English common law and New York courts consider the rivers and streams of our state as "public highways" if they are navigable.

As a landowner living on the banks of a popular recreation stream in New York State, I sometimes wish I could keep people from floating past my house, especially when they're dragging beer coolers behind innertubes and yelling to friends as they party the afternoon away and disturb everyone on the river. After all I own the land that borders the stream and the land under it, so why can't I block off my section of stream when I feel like it?

Simple. New York State law says I cannot.

Long before there were roads, waterways were the routes of travel. English common law and New York courts consider the rivers and streams of our state as "public highways" if they are navigable.

"Ah Ha!", say some streamside landowners,"there's the rub. The stream near my house is not navigable, not a single boat could get through the shallow water or all those rocks."

Well, let's see what the courts have said about that.

Way back in 1866 the New York Court of Appeals (Morgan v. King, 35 NY 453) expressed the common law right thusly:

The true rule is, that the public have a right of way in every stream which is capable, in its natural state and its ordinary volume of water, of transporting, in a condition fit for market, the products of the forests or mines, or of the tillage of the soil upon its banks.

Of course this ruling by itself left many interpretations of just what *capable, natural state, ordinary volume, transporting* and *navigable* meant, so the Court added that if a body of water would float to market even "single logs or sticks of timber" it **was navigable**.

Further guidance on the characteristics of navigable waters was provided by the Court of Appeals in the Morgan decision:

Nor is it necessary, that the stream should be capable of being thus navigated, against the current, as well as in the direction of its current. If it is so far navigable or floatable, in its natural state and its ordinary capacity, as to be of public use in the transportation of property, the public claim to such use ought to be liberally supported.

Nor is it essential to the easement, that the capacity of the stream, as above defined, should be continuous, or in other words, that the ordinary state, at all seasons of the year, should be such as to make it navigable. If it is ordinarily subject to periodical fluctuations in the volume and height of its water, attributable to natural causes, and recurring as regularly as the seasons, and if its periods of high water or navigable capacity, ordinarily, continue a sufficient length of time to make it useful as a highway, it is subject to the public easement.

So, if the stream you plan to canoe-fish can—and has—floated logs during the spring runoff, it's considered navigable waters and you have the right to canoe it without interference from landowners. That, as you might well imagine, includes just about every major and most minor stream in the state. All of the 25 rivers and streams we canoe-fished come under that category.

There's more.

According to a Memorandum from Marc Gerstman, Deputy Commissioner and General Counsel, New York State Department of Environmental Conservation (DEC), dated May 9, 1991:

Generally, a legal right of use includes all incidental uses that are reasonably necessary in order to enjoy the right. As to waters which are navigable in fact, these incidental uses would include poling or lining through rapids and otherwise touching the streambed incident to navigation, walking ahead to scout rapids, and carrying or portaging a vessel on the shore or margin of the waterway to the minimum extent necessary to go around or avoid obstacles. In connection with the latter, the fact that some portions of a stream are non-navigable does not preclude a determination that the stream is navigable as a whole.

There is also authority that the public has a right to fish from a boat in navigable waters, even if the bed of the stream is in private ownership, subject to applicable DEC fishing regulations. However, no cases have held that this includes a right to get out of the boat to wade around to fish, or a right to fish from the bank.

*The public right of navigation does **not** include a right to camp or picnic on privately owned land, nor to cross privately-owned land to gain access to or egress from navigable waters.*

So, it's the law that you can canoe, portage when necessary and **fish from the canoe** on the rivers and streams of New York without landowner interference.

And if the landowner does interfere? According to the DEC Memorandum noted above:

*... the courts have held that it is a **public** nuisance for a landowner to obstruct, annoy or hinder right of passage on privately owned navigable waters; public nuisances are generally actionable only by the state absent a showing of special damages suffered by a private party.*

Presently there are "exceptions" to these laws and rulings, but they apply to only a few streams in the Adirondack Mountains. Influential and wealthy landowners who own thousands of acres of land have blocked passage on some Adrirondack waters since before the turn of the century and wish to continue that practice in the future. Their rights to do so have been tested and are being argued in the courts.

Parts of Beaver River and Moose River are included in these contested "exceptions" to the rights of passage. While neither of these rivers are among the 25 we canoe-fished, they are listed as additional streams to canoe-fish in the northern region.

It is very important to note that the rights of passage on rivers and streams that run through private property, **do not** include the right of access or the right to fish from shore or by wading. Unless the landowner has sold the fishing rights (see Fishing Rights) along the stream, he can ban or restrict access and use of the streambank.

Once you and your canoe are on the river or stream, you can fish it. Finding access isn't too difficult on most New York streams. In some areas special access sites are provided by the state and local governments. Generally, the state, county or city owns the land near bridges and roads that run next to the water, so access is usually permitted in these areas.

The "Rights of Passage" are yours, but with those rights comes the responsibility and obligation to respect the rights of landowners —private and public. Among other things that means doing everything possible to keep our rivers and streams clean and undisturbed.

APPENDIX TWO

FISHING RIGHTS

Since 1935 New York State has purchased 1200 miles of Public Fishing Rights on more than 350 coldwater and warmwater streams.

There are 70,000 miles of rivers and streams in New York State. While some of these waters pass through state lands, most of them flow through private lands. Many landowners post their streamside property so fishing from shore or wading is prohibited. Canoe-fishermen—once on the water—can fish these streams (see Rights of Passage) from the canoe, however, there is no getting around the fact that the best way, and sometimes the only way, to fish some areas is by wading.

Thanks to the New York State Fishing Rights Program portions of hundreds of rivers and streams that run through private lands are open to fishing from shore and by wading. Access to these areas are provided at designated Fishermen Parking Areas and the stretches of stream open to fishing are posted with "Public Fishing" signs every 300 feet along the shoreline. One of the best publications I've found to locate these "Fishing Rights" waters in every area of the state is the "I Love New York, Bass, Walleye, Pike, Panfish and Musky Fishing" brochure available from the New York State DEC. It features regional maps that highlight Public Fishing Streams —- including trout streams. More detailed information can be obtained from your local DEC office. Addresses for ordering DEC brochures are listed in the "Other Sources of Information" appendix.

IT ALL STARTED 60 YEARS AGO

Sixty years ago New York sportsmen urged the then New York State Conservation Department to develop a program to purchase the fishing rights on the better trout waters throughout the state. Since this Fishing Rights Program began in 1935 New York State has purchased 1200 miles of public fishing rights on more than 350 coldwater and warmwater streams.

Over the years the purchases of fishing rights have ebbed and flowed, depending on available funds, and on the enthusiasm of sportsmen, landowners and the state personnel who administered the program. Prime waters on such streams as the Delaware and the Willowemoc in the Catskills; the Ausable and the Saranac in the Adirondacks; West Canada Creek and Fish Creek in central New York; Catherine Creek and the Cohocton River in the Finger Lakes area; the Genesee River and Cattaraugus Creek in the western region, and sections of fishing streams in almost every area of the state came under the New York State Fishing Rights Program.

THOUSANDS OF MILES OF STREAMS ARE ELIGIBLE

There are literally thousands of miles of streams that could come under this program. The fact is that because of New York's pure waters laws there are many more streams that qualify today than there were in 1935. AND, while this program has concentrated on trout water in the past, in recent years warmwater streams that offer bass, walleye and pike fishing have been included.

VALUE TO THE LANDOWNER

It has never been easy to convince landowners to sell the state the fishing rights to their lands, but there are many benefits to such arrangements. Some landowners want their streamside property to remain as wild as possible for as long as possible. By selling the fishing rights to the state they can insure that their streamside lands will never be developed. The sale of fishing rights is a permanent easement which will apply to all future owners. The easement restricts building or fencing (except for cattle fences) within 33 feet of the stream and gives the public permanent permission to travel along the bank to fish.

Many landowners who own streamside property do not realize that they cannot sell their property—now or in the future—as home or other building sites because their lands are in the **100 YEAR FLOOD ZONE**. This little known restriction, required by federal law, makes it impossible to get a mortgage to build along most New York rivers and streams. These landowners can benefit financially by selling the fishing rights and can continue to use their land for all normal purposes such as farming, grazing, lumbering, water supply and of course fishing.

The state pays up to $25,000 per mile (both sides) for a high value stream and as low as $3,000 per mile for a low-value streams. Payments for less than a mile or for one side of the stream are based on the per mile rate. It's a one-time payment.

Fishing rights property can be posted against hunting or any other type of trespass if posters make it clear that fishing is allowed along the waterway and its banks where the easement is sold.

The state, depending on available resources, also provides stream improvement including bank protection and erosion control, plus fisheries management that includes stocking the streams where fishing rights are purchased. This of course improves fishing for everyone.

Another benefit to landowners is that Environmental Conservation Officers (ECO'S) pay special attention to fishing rights property.

HERE'S HOW

The New York State Department of Environmental Conservation (DEC) administers this program. Their Fisheries Division already has a list of possible stream-rights properties and they are very interested in hearing about new prospects.

Landowners can contact DEC at any of the 17 regional and sub offices or at the Albany office. In many cases DEC can tell which land is in the 100 Year Flood Zone by consulting the Flood Zone Maps they have on file. Some landowners will have to contact their local zoning board for that information.

Sportsmen can act on their own to locate landowners who are interested in selling the fishing rights to their streamside property, but an organizational effort is often more productive. In either case a visit to the nearest DEC office will help to identify waters that meet the criteria and introduce you to local personnel who are familiar with the program.

Sportsmen organizations can invite local DEC fisheries personnel to club meetings to discuss the program. Such a discussion could start a club activity that would be a major contribution to the future of fishing.

ADOPT A STREAM IN YOUR AREA

A few sportsmen's organizations have adopted streams in their area. In addition to cleaning up the stream and reporting polluters to authorities, they encourage landowners to sell the fishing rights on their streamside property.

The Sauquoit Creek Fish and Game Club in central New York transformed their namesake from one of the most polluted, trash strewn waterways in the state to prime trout water. It took more than a decade of determination and a great deal of bull work to re-create the creek's trout habitat.

At the same time these sportsmen were cleaning up Sauquoit Creek they were talking to landowners about selling the fishing rights to the state. Their efforts have helped guarantee fishermen access to almost six miles of trout water. Today this relatively small tributary to the Mohawk River is an excellent example of what sportsmen can do when they **adopt a stream**.

WHERE DOES THE MONEY COME FROM?

Bond Acts have provided most of the money for the purchase of fishing rights. Funds were allocated for this purpose in a 1972 Bond Act, and DEC has only recently depleted those funds. Incidentally, there was a great deal of money appropriated in a 1986 Bond Act that could have been used to purchase stream rights, but it was used for other land acquisitions because it just wasn't needed for the Fishing Rights Program at the time. Presently there are only a few thousand dollars available for purchasing fishing rights.

WHAT ABOUT THE FUTURE?

Future money? There is no guarantee that there will be other sources of funds for this program, but New York sportsmen have paid their own way for a couple of hundred years. Perhaps when they realize that the Fishing Rights Program can continue to guarantee the rights to fish more rivers and streams in New York State, they will find a way to pay for it. It would be a shame to see it all end after 60 years of success.

APPENDIX THREE

HOW EASY IS IT TO TIP A CANOE?

I've been canoeing for more than 30 years. I am not an expert canoeist, far from it, but I have canoed through wild rapids and across white-capped lakes. I've been pushed against trees on high-water streams, hung up on submerged rocks and logs, and nearly swamped by power boats. I've tipped over in a canoe—by accident—only twice. Both times were in quiet water.

Some 30 years ago a fishing buddy and I launched my old wide-bottomed fiberglass canoe on a small pond in upstate New York where we heard there were some big largemouths. As we paddled around the pond and saw more and more big bass swimming in the weeds, we got excited. We got more excited when one of them took my popper off the surface.

After I boated that first fish of the day, my partner stood up in the front of the canoe so he could see where the really big bass were. When he saw a monster he guessed to be at least seven pounds, halfway across the pond, he frantically tried to paddle with one hand while holding his rod in the other. He lost his balance, fell and tipped the canoe over.

As soon as we surfaced he started apologizing. Heh, the water was warm, no one was hurt and he looked a sight—hair plastered on his head, water dripping off his nose—so I started laughing. He did the same, grabbed a floating paddle and climbed up on the upside down canoe. I grabbed the two floating poppers and wound the fishing lines around my wrist. He paddled and I kicked for shore. It took awhile to realize we were going nowhere. The anchor had fallen to the bottom and was holding fast. I found the anchor line, pulled it tight, gave it a tug and wound a couple of feet around my other wrist. In a couple of minutes we were righting the canoe and looking for our fishing rods and tackle. We found everything except his tackle pouch that contained a supply of heavy sinkers.

That experience didn't keep me or my fishing buddies from standing up in a canoe, but it did make me realize that anytime someone stands up in a canoe they should be prepared to get wet.

For almost 30 years I prided myself in the fact that despite some close calls, I had never again gone over in a canoe. As far as I was concerned a canoe was a very forgiving watercraft. My canoe found its way through rapids, bounced off boulders, rode the waves on wind-tossed lakes and always went out if its way to keep me safe and dry. Every other canoe I fished from for 30 years did the same. I was completely confident that a wide-bottomed canoe was almost as stable—and far more forgiving—than a flat-bottomed boat. I couldn't understand why anyone would be afraid to fish from a canoe.

Two years ago, while I was well into writing this book, I bought a 16-foot Mad River Explorer, kevlar canoe. It was—and is—what dreams are made of: light weight, a mere 53 pounds; red in color with natural wood trim, beautiful and great for photographs; a wide shallow V bottom (See Chapter 1), perfect for paddling long distances and going upstream to retrieve lures. I grew to love that canoe and used it to canoe-fish streams throughout New York State.

My son-in-law, Mark Nicholson had never been in a canoe, so I offered to introduce him to canoeing on West Canada Creek in mid-May. I was honored actually. Mark was a Naval officer. He had captained ships on two oceans. He was also an exercise fanatic who ran everyday and worked out while watching television or reading the paper. He had run some of the most grueling races on the east and west coast, including the Marine Corps and San Francisco and Los Angeles marathons. He did everything with enthusiasm.

While we drove up to the launch site I asked Mark if he had ever had a paddle in his hand. He said he had paddled life rafts. I jokingly noted that a canoe is not as stable as a life raft. After we unloaded the canoe and our gear, I grabbed a paddle and demonstrated the basic forward and reverse paddle strokes that would allow us to maneuver the canoe down the river. Although I hardly ever use it, I included a demonstration of the "draw" stroke. Reaching out from the side of the canoe with the paddle and "drawing" it back to the side of the canoe will turn the canoe faster than a back paddle.

Mark learned quickly and was soon doing most of the paddling from the front of the canoe while I fished. He learned to read the water faster than anyone I have ever introduced to canoeing. Must have been all his Navy training and experience.

It was a beautiful spring day. The sky was blue, flowers were blooming and fish were biting. Fact is, I caught the brook trout pictured on the back cover of this book and Mark used my camera to capture the moment before I released the fish.

An hour later we passed a pair of abutments that once held a covered bridge ... and almost always gave up a smallmouth bass to a spinning lure. My line was tangled, so I asked Mark if he could turn the canoe around so I could make a couple casts. As he reached out with the paddle, I prepared to let the lure fly. Next thing I knew I was under the water and not touching bottom.

We surfaced about the same time, taking deep breaths, shocked by the cold water. Mark pulled the canoe to shore while I grabbed as many items as I could find that were floating near the canoe. We had flipped over so fast, many items, including one of my fishing rods and a paddle, were still in the canoe when we turned it right side up. My camera was in a bag looped around my neck. I got out of the water so fast it never got wet. We retrieved everything but my ball cap and one fishing rod.

Mark had applied his strength and enthusiasm to a draw stroke with such gusto that it didn't stop at the side of the canoe, but continued under the canoe ... and literally forced it over. Except for losing a new fishing rod, getting a sunburn where my hat should have been, getting wet and cold, and looking like a couple of drowned rats, we were no worse for the experience.

Actually, it turned out, I was better for the experience. It took several trips in that canoe before I really felt comfortable in it. Now I understand why some fishermen are afraid to fish from a canoe. I also vowed to never again teach anyone the draw stroke. I removed all reference to it in the chapter that explains how to handle a canoe.

So, how easy is it to tip a canoe. It's not. In fact it's difficult to tip a wide-bottomed canoe completely over. Usually it takes something stupid—like standing up and trying to paddle with one hand, or something extreme—like a powerful sideways, under the canoe paddle stroke—to do it. But just knowing it can be done has made me a little more careful and a lot more considerate. When I canoe-fish with someone who has never been in a canoe or is uncomfortable canoeing, I start them out in my Sportspal. I call it my "barge" because it's so stable. After that, I'll use my Mad River Explorer so they can get the feel of a "real" canoe.

Incidentally, Mark and I ran a good rapids in that same canoe the following year and didn't even come close to tipping over. Of course I'll never let him forget that he ruined my 30-year record.

APPENDIX FOUR
CANOE-CAMPING EQUIPMENT

❏ **Tent/poles**
❏ **Plastic tarps**
❏ **Sleeping bags**
❏ **Sleeping mats**
❏ **Back packs**
❏ **Lantern**
❏ **Stove**
❏ **Cooler(s)**
❏ **Hatchet / saw**
❏ **Trowel / shovel**
❏ **Water filter/pump**

COOKING STUFF
❏ grill
❏ stove
❏ coffee pot
❏ cooking kit
❏ fry pan
❏ spatula
❏ tongs
❏ mess kits
❏ utensils
❏ soap for dishes
❏ brillo pad
❏ paper towels
❏ aluminum foil
❏ zip lock bags

CLOTHING
❏ waterproof boots
❏ camp shoes or sneakers
❏ waterproof socks
❏ rain suit
❏ down vest
❏ extra pants
❏ long johns
❏ extra wool socks
❏ chamois shirt
❏ wool shirt/jacket
❏ extra underwear
❏ handkerchief
❏ knit cap
❏ gloves

PERSONAL STUFF
❏ day packs
❏ knife
❏ compass & maps
❏ canteen
❏ flashlight
❏ first aid kit
❏ aspirin / antacid
❏ sterno / candles
❏ matches / lighter
❏ tape / twine / wire
❏ duct tape
❏ camera/film
❏ fishing rods / tackle
❏ notebook / pens
❏ toilet paper
❏ hand soap
❏ toothbrush / paste
❏ water tablets

FOOD
❏ trail mix
❏ pancake mix
❏ coffee
❏ sugar / creamer
❏ tang
❏ hot chocolate
❏ margarine
❏ syrup
❏ salt / pepper
❏ onions
❏ bread
❏ potatoes
❏ frozen meat
❏ frozen meal
❏ frozen breakfast sausage
❏ eggs or egg beaters
❏ bread
❏ crackers
❏ cookies (oreos, etc.)
❏ freeze dried noodle dinner
❏ oatmeal
❏ chocolate candy
❏ cheese

APPENDIX FIVE
OTHER SOURCES OF INFORMATION

Maps

**Available at Book Stores,
Sportshops and/or mail order**

Road Maps
New York State Atlas & Gazetteer
De Lorme Mapping Co.
PO Box 298
Freeport, Maine 04031
also available from
Northwoods Publications, Inc.
PO Box 90, Lemoyne, PA 17043
$14.95 plus $2.00 shipping and handling:(1995 prices)

Stream Maps
(includes information on fish species)
New York Stream Map & Location Guide
Vivid Publishing, Inc.
PO Box 1572, Williamsport, PA 17703
Mail order and current prices call
1-*800-787-3267*

Topographical Maps
New York State Topographical Maps
U.S. Geological Survey
Reston, Virginia 22092

*New York State
County Road Maps*
available from
County Highway Departments

New York Sportsman Magazine
*Past Issues That Featured Centerfold
Canoe-Fishing Maps*
Oct 1981 . . . . .UNADILLA RIVER
Oct 1984 . . . . .PECONIC RIVER
Oct 1987 . . . . . .CHENANGO RIVER
Oct 1991 . . . . .GRASSE RIVER
Feb 1993 . . .WEST CANADA CREEK
Feb 1994 . .UPPER GENESEE RIVER
Feb 1995 . . . . .BLACK RIVER
Mar 1995 . . . . . .DELAWARE RIVER
$5.00 each from:
PAST ISSUES,
NEW YORK SPORTSMAN
BOX A, PROSPECT, NY 13435

Books

**Available at Book Stores
and Libraries**

The Canoer's Bible
   by Mead/Fears
The Basic Essentials of Canoeing
   by Cliff Jacobson
Canoeing Central New York
   by William P. Ehling
The Inland Fishes of New York State
   by C. Lavett Smith
*Freshwater Fishes of New York State
-A Field Guide*
   by Robert G. Werner
*McClane's New Standard Fishing
Encyclopedia*
   by A. J. McClane

Booklets and Pamphlets

New York State Fishing & Regulation Guide—where fishing licenses are sold.

Fishing and Canoeing the Grasse River
Fishing and Canoeing the Indian River
Fishing and Canoeing the Oswegatchie River
The Raquette River in St. Lawrence County
Order from: Regional Fisheries Manager, NYSDEC, 317 Washington St. Watertown, NY 13601-3787

I Love New York Bass, Walleye, Pike, Panfish and Musky Fishing
I Love New York Trout and Salmon Fishing
New York State Boat Launch Sites
Order from: NYS DEC, 50 Wolf Road, Albany, NY 12233

Upper Delaware River
  Scenic and Recreation River
  Visitor Information Guide

Upper Delaware River
  Official Map and Guide
Order from: National Park Service, POB C (CFB), Narrowsburg, NY 12764

I Love New York Travel Guide
  and Tourism Map
Order from: Division of Tourism, One Commerce Plaza, Albany, NY 12245

Annual Directory
  Licensed Guides of New York State
Order from: NYSOGA, POB 4704, Queensbury, NY 12804

Canoes and Canoe Equipment Manufacturers

Coleman Canoes, Coleman Co., 250 N. St Francis, Wichita, KS 67201

Grumman Canoes, Grumman Boats, POB 449, Marathon, NY 13803

Hornbeck Canoes, Hornbeck Boats, Box 23, Troutbrook Rd., Olmsteadville, NY 12857

Mad River Canoes, Mad River Canoe Co., PO Box 610, Waitsfield, VT 05673

Old Town Canoes, Old Town Canoe Co., 58 Middle St., Old Town, ME 04468

Sportspal Canoes, Meyers Boat Company, 543 Lawrence St., Adrian, MI 49221

Canoe Pack Baskets, Natural Bridge Basket, POB 254, Natural Bridge, NY 13665

Canoe-Fishing Notes

Canoe-Fishing Notes

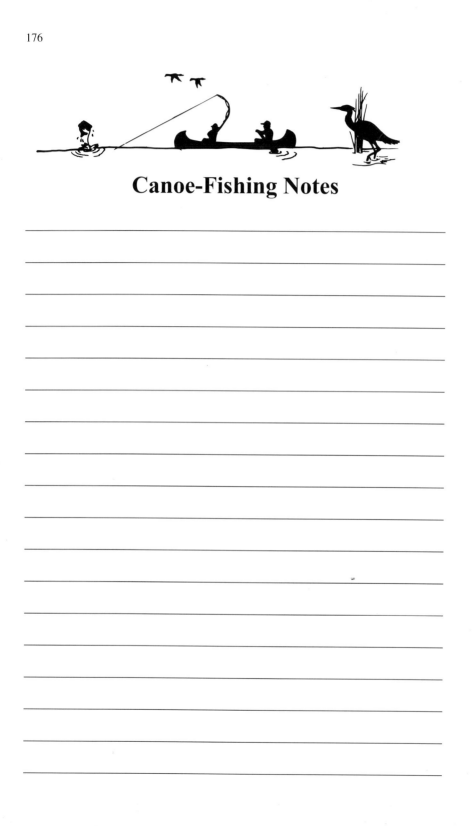

Canoe-Fishing Notes